A Roman Verse Satire Reader

Selections from Lucilius, Horace, Persius, and Juvenal

Catherine C. Keane

Bolchazy-Carducci Publishers, Inc.
Mundelein, Illinois USA

ℬ𝓬 LATIN Readers

These readers provide well annotated Latin selections written by experts in the field, to be used as authoritative introductions to Latin authors, genres, topics, or themes for intermediate or advanced college Latin study. Their relatively small size (covering 500–600 lines) makes them ideal to use in combination. Each volume includes a comprehensive introduction, bibliography for further reading, Latin text with notes at the back, and complete vocabulary. Nineteen volumes are currently scheduled for publication; others are under consideration. Check our website for updates: www.BOLCHAZY.com.

Series Editor: Ronnie Ancona

Volume Editor: Laurie Haight Keenan

Cover Design & Typography: Adam Phillip Velez

Map: Mapping Specialists, Inc.

A Roman Verse Satire Reader
Selections from Lucilius, Horace, Persius, and Juvenal

Catherine C. Keane

© 2010 Bolchazy-Carducci Publishers, Inc.
All rights reserved.

Bolchazy-Carducci Publishers, Inc.
1570 Baskin Road
Mundelein, Illinois 60060
www.bolchazy.com

Printed in the United States of America
2010
by United Graphics

ISBN 978-0-86516-685-1

Library of Congress Cataloging-in-Publication Data

A Roman verse satire reader : selections from Lucilius, Horace, Persius, and Juvenal /
Catherine C. Keane.
   p. cm. -- (BC latin readers)
  Includes bibliographical references.
  Text in Latin; introduction, notes, and commentary in English.
  ISBN 978-0-86516-685-1 (pbk. : alk. paper) 1. Verse satire, Latin. I. Keane, Catherine.
PA6134.R66 2010
871'.070801--dc22

                                                      2010008226

Contents

List of Illustrations vi

Preface vii

Introduction ix

Latin Text 1

Lucilius, SATIRES

Scenes from a gladiatorial match,
    Satires, fragments 172–75, 176–81, 185. 1

Human superstition, *Satires*, fragments 524–29 2

The Roman rat-race, *Satires*, fragments 1145–51. 2

A definition of virtue, *Satires*, fragments 1196–1208. 2

Horace, SATIRES

Greed and its manifestations, *Satire* 1.1.41–79 3

Horace defends his satire, *Satire* 1.4.103–43 4

How to hunt legacies, *Satire* 2.5.23–50 6

The satirist in the hot seat, *Satire* 2.7.21–71. 7

The satirist in the hot seat (continued),
    Satire 2.7.111–18 9

Persius, SATIRES

A self-sufficient satirist, *Satire* 1.1–12 9

A self-sufficient satirist (continued),
    Satire 1.107–34 10

Foolish prayers, *Satire* 2.1–16. 11

Foolish prayers (continued), *Satire* 2.31–51. 12

The satirist's philosophical and ethical roots,
    Satire 5.21–51 12

Juvenal, SATIRES

Identifying a crisis, *Satire* 1.63–93 14

Identifying a crisis (continued), *Satire* 1.135–46 15

Trials of the urban poor, *Satire* 3.190–231 15

Unchaste women on display, *Satire* 6.60–102 17

The scandal of performing nobles,
    Satire 8.183–99 19

The scandal of performing nobles (continued),
    Satire 8.215–30 19

The good old days, *Satire* 13.38–70 20

Parents who teach vice, *Satire* 14.1–55 21

Commentary 25

Lucilius, SATIRES

Scenes from a gladiatorial match,
    Satires, fragments 172–75, 176–81, 185 25

Human superstition, *Satires*, fragments 524–29 27

The Roman rat-race, *Satires*, fragments 1145–51 28

A definition of virtue, *Satires*, fragments 1196–1208 29

Horace, SATIRES

Greed and its manifestations, *Satire* 1.1.41–79 31

Horace defends his satire, *Satire* 1.4.103–43 37

How to hunt legacies, *Satire* 2.5.23–50 41

The satirist in the hot seat, *Satire* 2.7.21–71 44

The satirist in the hot seat (continued),
    Satire 2.7.111–18 51

Persius, SATIRES

   A self-sufficient satirist, *Satire* 1.1–12 52

   A self-sufficient satirist (continued),
      Satire 1.107–34 54

   Foolish prayers, *Satire* 2.1–16. 59

   Foolish prayers (continued), *Satire* 2.31–51. 62

   The satirist's philosophical and ethical roots,
      Satire 5.21–51 64

Juvenal, SATIRES

   Identifying a crisis, *Satire* 1.63–93 68

   Identifying a crisis (continued), *Satire* 1.135–46 73

   Trials of the urban poor, *Satire* 3.190–231 75

   Unchaste women on display, *Satire* 6.60–102. 81

   The scandal of performing nobles,
      Satire 8.183–99 86

   The scandal of performing nobles (continued),
      Satire 8.215–30 90

   The good old days, *Satire* 13.38–70 93

   Parents who teach vice, *Satire* 14.1–55 98

Illustration Credits 104

Vocabulary 105

List of Illustrations

1. Portion of William R. Shepherd's plan of
    Imperial Rome xxii

2. Map: Locations in Roman Italy mentioned
    in the texts and notes 24

3. Graffito of victorious gladiator carrying palm
    branch (Pompeii, Imperial period) 26

4. Terracotta figurines of two comic actors
    playing a male slave and a *paterfamilias*
    (Etruria, Republican period) 38

5. Terracotta group of two women conversing
    (Asia Minor, Hellenistic period) 83

Preface

This reader provides instructors of advanced undergraduate Latin students with representative selections from the work of the Roman verse satirists Lucilius, Horace, Persius, and Juvenal. The selections and commentary will illustrate for students the thematic coherence and development of the satiric genre, while acquainting them with the individual poets' distinct styles and themes.

For the fragments of Lucilius I have used Warmington's Loeb Classical Library text (Revised ed., 1967). For Horace, Persius, and Juvenal I have used the Oxford texts of Wickham (2nd ed., ed. Garrod, 1922) and Clausen (Revised ed., 1992). See the Preface to the text for notes on the small changes I have made. Macrons in the Vocabulary follow Smith and Lockwood's *Chambers Murray Latin-English Dictionary* (New York, 1976). Two abbreviations are used in references in the notes: GL, for *Gildersleeve's Latin Grammar*; and B, for *Bennett's New Latin Grammar*.

I am grateful to the Latin Reader Series Editor, Ronnie Ancona, for originally soliciting this book and for providing advice from the proposal stage through completion of the work. Both she and Laurie Haight Keenan at Bolchazy-Carducci read through the manuscript meticulously and patiently, as did two anonymous readers. Any errors and infelicities that remain are my own. I thank everyone at the press who gave me much-needed help with preparation of the text and images. Barbara McManus and Ann Raia Colaneri graciously allowed me to use their photographs at no charge. My student assistant at Washington University, Shana Zaia, took on the long and laborious task of preparing the Vocabulary; she performed this and various other proofing and formatting tasks carefully and conscientiously. I was able to test a first draft of the commentary in a seminar on Roman satire in the fall of 2008. I am grateful to that lively group of eleven fine students for their feedback and their enthusiasm about the project.

I dedicate this book to the memory of my professor Bob Palmer. His wit has often been on my mind during my work on this project, but I have also tried to follow his equally memorable standards of precision.

CATHERINE C. KEANE
St. Louis, Missouri

Introduction

❧ Overview

Quintilian, the famous Roman professor of the first century CE, called satire "entirely ours" (*tota nostra*; *Education of the Orator* 10.1.93). Whether he meant that the genre was a Roman invention or just that it was perfectly designed to appeal to Roman readers, he could not have anticipated that two thousand years later, non-Roman students and scholars would have the opportunity to use satiric poems as a window into Roman culture. Satire makes entertaining and challenging material for Latin students at all levels. The genre's authors were witnesses to the spectacular growth of Roman political and military power, the expansion and diversification of Roman society, and the evolution of a wide spectrum of Roman literary genres. Satire is a kind of response to these developments. It documents daily life and customs, reflects on historical events and figures, and articulates and scrutinizes particularly Roman values.

Consequently, satire's content is generally accessible and appealing to Latin students. Most of the genre's challenges come—along with many pleasures—in its rhetoric and style. The poets' Latin is lexically rich and stylistically varied, ranging from colloquial to grand in order to fit different subjects and agendas. Their work is influenced by many kinds of Roman discourse: other literary genres, such as epic poetry and comic drama; other intellectual pursuits of the Roman elite, such as moral philosophy and rhetoric; and the real-life dramas of politics and law. But the satirists, in turn, make their own provocative contributions to the conversation in all these areas.

॰ *Characteristics of the genre*

The verse satires of Lucilius, Horace, Persius, and Juvenal together constitute a distinct tradition characterized by a consistent meter and similar themes and rhetorical strategies. Within this formal framework, however, there is much variety in subject-matter and style. This quality goes back to satire's murky origins in a lost collection of poems by Ennius (239–169 BCE), who is best known for his tragic and epic compositions. Judging by the few remaining fragments (quotations by later authors), Ennius' *Saturae* were a motley assortment of poems in different meters and dealing with a range of different subjects, but mainly emphasizing everyday life and featuring the author (or, more accurately, a cultivated authorial persona) as a character. Ennius' title for the collection seems to imply that variety was its dominant and unifying characteristic. *Satura* is a mysterious word: it looks like the Latin adjective meaning "stuffed" in its feminine singular form, although it comes with no noun attached. But interpreted loosely, it applies well to Ennius' work and the later satiric texts we possess.

This apparent sense of the genre's name seems to have influenced Ennius' successors, who make satire a literally "stuffed" genre by frequently using food and dining as themes. This is a clever angle to adopt partly because scenes of eating and discussions of food can be windows into human character and morals (e.g., **Horace *Satire* 1.1.41–79** and **Juvenal 1.135–41**). But the dining theme helps the satirists flesh out their genre's identity in other ways as well. Food anecdotes and language support the poets' regular claims that satire is a mundane, even sub-literary genre concerned with everyday life. This image is belied by the satirists' intricate art (including, ironically, their use of culinary metaphors to convey ideas about their poetry; e.g., **Persius 1.125** and **Juvenal 1.86**). Despite this, the poets evidently want their readers to entertain the idea of satire's "low" status as they explore the genre's various forms. Lucilius and Horace can claim merely to be "chatting" with their readers (they both use the term *sermo* to describe their work), while they skillfully adapt conventions from Roman comedy and other poetry. Similarly,

Persius' ostensibly private and philosophically themed talk is made up partly of complex literary borrowings, and Juvenal advertises his first book of satire both as an artless emotional catharsis and a grand moralistic work in the style of epic poetry.

Students using this volume will benefit by familiarizing themselves with some issues in satiric scholarship and discussing the individual selections in these terms. It should first be noted that each of the satirists wrote at least one apologia or explicitly "programmatic" poem, in which he describes and defends his agenda in writing satire and envisions a backlash from offended readers. Each poet borrows some programmatic strategies and themes from his predecessor(s), while designing an argument that applies uniquely to his own work. A significant element in programmatic satire—and indeed throughout all satire—is the authorial persona, literally a "mask" through which the poet speaks and which may exhibit attitudes and characteristics such as irony, boorishness, or anger. The satirists, like all other educated Roman men, had all studied literary drama and rhetoric in school, and had also learned how to construct personae for their own "performances." In reading satiric poems we may prefer just to call the persona the author's "personality." If we use this term, however, we should remain aware that this personality, when deployed in poetry, is fundamentally an artificial dramatic creation (whether or not it resembles the historical poet).

Ancient readers familiar with the type characters of comic drama and the conventions of performed rhetoric would have been alert to the expressions and speech patterns that indicate what sort of persona is being used in any given work. For modern readers, a poet's persona may or may not make such an immediate impact. But even when its presence is subtle, the persona does tend to affect how we evaluate individual satires, and more broadly to shape our ideas about the genre's proper tone and purpose. In fact, the Roman satirists appear to have had not one but several aims: for example, to criticize vices, to abuse individuals, to create humor and drama from the everyday and from abuse itself, and to convey moral and aesthetic lessons. Any given poem may appear to highlight one agenda over the other, especially if its persona is particularly critical, playful, or erudite.

The individual satirists are best known for the personae they used most frequently and strikingly, and in this volume Lucilius' trademark exuberance, Horace's gentleness, Persius' abrasiveness, and Juvenal's vehemence are represented well. But the selections also show that each poet did not confine himself to a single persona or style. It is always important to consider each poem individually—to ask how the speaker is trying to make us see him, and how this relates to the subject-matter of the poem. Some satires, especially programmatic ones, seem fundamentally to be "about" the personality of the satirist himself. But even poems of this sort also explore morality and aesthetics, overtly or cryptically. The satirist figure is never outside the world his satire describes and criticizes, but a part of it. To point to an example, **Horace** turns the practicing satirist into a central subject of satire by presenting his first programmatic poem, *Satire* **1.4,** nearly at the middle of his first book, and by following this with additional "autobiographical" poems that weave the poet's story into the moral and social world of contemporary Rome. Horace's second book goes even further to turn the satirist into an object of scrutiny: for instance, *Satire* **2.7** shows us the poet allowing himself to become the target of criticism and ridicule. **Persius,** for his part, pretends to retreat from the public world at the end of *Satire* **1;** this is his way of signaling that he will write a very interior kind of satire, provoking himself and his readers to conduct a moral investigation of themselves instead of others (e.g., *Satire* **2** on prayer). Finding still another way to relate the satirist figure to his subjects, **Juvenal** tells us in *Satire* **1** that he writes down his satire while standing on the street corner; this suggests that he is a part of the world he depicts and even subject to the emotions he observes driving the people around him (**1.85–86**).

Outside of programmatic discussions, satire presents to the reader a wide range of rhetorical modes with their own patterns and functions. Among the passages selected for this volume are excerpts of narrative, dialogue, personal anecdotes, abstract moralizing, and narrative scenes of human behavior. Students will have many opportunities to compare satiric representations with other sources on Roman culture, and indeed to use the satirists' questions to investigate the reality. Many selections satirically portray quintessential

Roman institutions such as public shows, religion, slavery, dining, patronage, law, and education, as well as areas of private life such as personal ethics and family and marital relations. History and myth also play moderate roles in the satiric portrayal of Roman life and thought, as they do in many contemporary genres; students should recognize some familiar names.

∾ Authors, works, and passages in this volume

Ennius' *Saturae* were a poetic experiment by one of the founding fathers of Roman literature, rather than a new genre consciously introduced to Roman readers. It is a later author, Gaius **Lucilius**, who is called satire's "inventor" (Horace *Satire* 1.10.48). Lucilius came from Suessa Aurunca in southwest Italy (see map). He lived and wrote during the second half of the second century BCE, dividing his time between Rome and his estates in Italy and Sicily. He died in Naples in 102, having written thirty books of satiric poems. Although these were read with enthusiasm for centuries after the author's death, they ultimately survived only in fragments totaling about 1,300 lines. Lucilius seems to have followed the spirit of Ennius' *Saturae* to an extent. The fragments teem with mundane images of food, entertainment, sex, household management, and social interaction. Much of this seems to be centered on the satirist and his friends, among whom conversation is never just mundane; it also runs to literary and linguistic topics as well as politics. Thanks in part to the state of the text, variety reigns. But even in the scattered lines, we can see the qualities for which Lucilius was long admired: pointed and irreverent social criticism (e.g., **fragments 524–29** and **1145–51**), a lively and fluent style (**172–81** and **185, 1196–1208**), and a distinctive and down-to-earth authorial persona. Quintilian, in his evaluation of the satirists cited above, declares that Lucilius has "amazing erudition and outspokenness, and from that acerbity and plenty of wit" (*Education of the Orator* 10.1.94). All three later satirists in this volume name Lucilius as their first model (see **Persius Satire 1.114–15** and cf. especially Horace *Satires* 2.1 and Juvenal 1.19–20 and 165–67), while aiming to surpass him in different respects.

Lucilius' literary experiment had a social and historical context, of course. The poet lived and wrote while Rome's power in the Mediterranean was expanding dramatically, and he must have observed with interest the many fruits and challenges generated by these circumstances. Ambitious men competed vigorously for lucrative political and military posts; the well-connected accumulated fabulous wealth; there was a great influx of foreign slaves, goods, and tastes into Rome and Italy; and the rural poor—traditionally seen as representing the ancient Roman way of life and values—were increasingly marginalized, politically and economically. Political and cultural debates concerning these developments would rage until the final days of the Republic. Lucilius had a front-row seat to many significant political careers, dramas, and scandals of the late second century. He was a friend of prominent politicians, including Scipio Aemilianus ("Scipio the Younger," who razed Carthage in 146 and subsequently played a major role in Roman foreign policy) and Gaius Laelius, a celebrated orator and advocate of Greek philosophers in Rome. Unsurprisingly, much contemporary political talk seems to have found its way into the world of Lucilius' *Satires.* For example, in one book the poet imagined the gods debating the proper sentence to give a corrupt senator, Cornelius Lentulus Lupus, after his death; in another, he presented a parodic narrative of the real, earthly trial of a corrupt provincial governor, Mucius Scaevola. Finally, the more everyday dramas of business and social dealings in Rome itself are also represented, as in the abstract but vivid picture of the forum (**1145–51**).

Lucilius' perspective in the *Satires* reflects his socioeconomic position. Although he eschewed a political career himself, he was a member of the elite class that produced politicians, and in dramatizing typical goings-on and conversations of the day he does not give us much sense of the viewpoints or interests of non-elites. All the same, for later authors he became an emblem of irreverent free speech. His posthumous image is colored by the fact that he wrote during the heyday of the Republican government, a time idealized by many who saw frightening examples of censorship and political revenge under the emperors. For his literary successors in the Imperial period, Lucilius represented not just satire's experimental origins but the freer atmosphere of the lost Republic (see, e.g., Horace *Satire* 2.1.62–74 and Juvenal 1.151–57). Other writers who composed satire in the politically tumultuous era between 100 and the 30s BCE (Horace names one, Varro of Atax; see *Satire* 1.10.46–47) might have made interesting additions to our already substantial record of this period had their works survived.

Another by-product of empire was the effort to cultivate a Roman national literature and to educate the elite to read and critically assess both Greek and Roman works. In demonstrating his own erudition (and even in mocking others who did the same) Lucilius shows that satire was, from the beginning, fertilized by literary movements as well as political and social conditions. In the ages of Lucilius' successors, the other Roman literary genres—epic, tragedy, comedy, oratory, historiography, philosophical dialogue, lyric and elegiac poetry—continued to flourish and evolve in new directions, and to influence satire. But satire had a unique status as a genre with no direct Greek model (cf. Quintilian's claim that it is "entirely ours"). The genre's authors may have self-consciously assigned themselves the task of exploring the particular social, political, and moral issues that occupied Romans as their place in the Mediterranean world changed.

Our next extant satirist, Quintus Horatius Flaccus (**Horace**; 65–68 BCE), is himself a document of his time, and in contrast to Lucilius with his inherited status, one of the most famous cases of social mobility in Rome. Horace's father was a freed slave from Apulia (see map) who evidently achieved financial success and sent his son to Rome for a first-rate education. As a young man, Horace made his way from the losing side in the conflict that followed Julius Caesar's assassination into an association with the victors. The patronage and friendship of Maecenas, advisor to Caesar's heir Octavian (later the emperor Augustus), became the framework for a long and illustrious poetic career, the climax of which was the well-known lyric *Odes*, but which began with the quite different *Epodes* and *Satires*. These two collections were published during the last few years of the 30s BCE.

The book of *Epodes* showcases one kind of "abuse" poetry, modeled on a range of Greek examples. The *Satires*, also known as the *Sermones* ("chats"), fill two books. The first book contains ten poems, arranged carefully to spin out an explanation of Horace's agenda and to suggest connections between topics (much like the highly polished *Eclogues* of Vergil, published a few years earlier). We first meet Horace as a voice only, delivering a series of lectures on moral topics. These book's first three poems are reminiscent of the moralistic monologues ("diatribes") favored by Greek street-philosophers of the Hellenistic period (323–31 BCE). But Horace's is a textual diatribe, displaying remarkable lexical variation and subtlety in composition; it reveals new ideas with each rereading. In ***Satire* 1.1.41–79**, we see Horace acting out his newly established agenda of "telling the truth with a laugh" (*ridentem dicere verum*, 1.1.24). This technique does not necessarily save the audience from pain or discomfort, for Horace's persona is a striking blend of genial and pushy. In **1.4.103–43**, Horace has moved on to discuss his satire itself, and specifically to defend his practice of moral correction with an appealing description of the moral instruction he received from his father. Having established his credentials as a pious son, Horace moves on to unfold more aspects of his life (or his persona's) in subsequent poems, revealing his connections with the powerful, delicately describing his negotiation of his own social ascent, and commenting obliquely on current political affairs (1.5, 1.6, 1.9). He concocts superficially light narratives that allude to the assassination of Julius Caesar (1.7), the clashes between his political heirs (1.5), and the program of urban renewal in Rome that followed years of civil war (1.8). There is room in all this for plenty of generic moral commentary "with a laugh," but the poems really tell a story about the circumstances of Horace's early career. The book then ends with another explicit discussion of satire on the literary level (1.10), and Horace claims his place as Lucilius' more aesthetically polished heir.

Horace's second book begins by delicately acknowledging an external political change: Caesar Octavian has recently become the sole ruler of the Roman Empire. In *Satire* 2.1, the poet discusses with a legal expert the social risks he is taking as a satirist. Although he expresses confidence that Caesar's favor will protect him, Horace hints that there is potential for repression under the new regime, and he follows up this programmatic poem with a number of satires that seem to bury trenchant criticism or attribute it to people other than the poet. In other words, Horace pretends to move to the sidelines for his own safety and let others practice satire (while in reality, of course, he is continuing to direct the show). Two devices Horace particularly favors are conversation between fictional characters (exemplified by the dialogue of Ulysses and Tiresias; see **2.5.23–50**) and dialogues in which he participates, but in a passive or marginal role (e.g., **2.7.21–71, 111–18;** cf. 2.3, 2.4, 2.6, 2.8). One smaller-scale example of indirect satire, beloved by modern readers, is the fable of the town mouse and the country mouse embedded in *Satire* 2.6 and narrated by a neighbor of Horace's. With the whole series of poems, Horace seems to write himself out of the role of satirist, even ending the book after eight poems instead of repeating the neat set of ten. While his passive pose is in fact disingenuous, it does remind us that Horace is indeed preparing to "retire" from this genre to try his hand at a very different one, and in a very different Rome. This satirist is best known for his *Odes,* which develop a patriotic theme; he also composed philosophically themed *Epistles* in hexameter and a hymn for Augustus' Secular Games. His hexameter *Art of Poetry* cemented his legacy as unofficial "national poet" of Augustan Rome after Vergil's death.

Satire was reinvented again in the Imperial period, while the last emperor from Augustus' family was in power (Nero, 54–68 CE). This was an age of extraordinary and diverse literary production in Rome, but also an age of censorship, when expressions of nostalgia for the Republic or praise of the emperor's opponents might get an author into trouble. Nero's increasing paranoia, and the development of a real plot against him, would claim the lives of the philosopher Seneca and the epic poet Lucan (both were compelled to commit suicide in 65). Like these and many other opponents of Nero, Aules **Persius** Flaccus (34–62 CE) was an adherent of Stoic philosophy, but his early death by a stomach illness kept him from a fate like theirs. Persius came from a wealthy family of Volterra, an Etruscan town (see map).

He studied with the famous Stoic Cornutus, who later helped edit the deceased poet's work: a single book of six hexameter *Satires* and an accompanying fourteen-line piece (informally known as the "prologue") in choliambic meter.

Persius is a poet first and a Stoic second, but his Stoicism had a significant and complex impact on his version of verse satire. Although there were plenty of scandals inside and outside the Imperial house during the infamous reign of Nero, Persius' poems focus mainly on the inner life and personal consequences of vice and folly. He does not "walk the streets" and criticize others as Horace (and later Juvenal) does, but recommends a kind of Stoic-inspired retreat, self-examination, and self-education that is meant to take a lifetime. Stoicism also influences Persius' use of language. The Stoics held that words "naturally" contained and conveyed ideas, and that speech and writing ought to make listeners and readers labor to tease out those ideas. Accordingly, Stoics favored raw and jarring expressions over smoothly flowing composition that might give aesthetic pleasure to its audience (like Horace's verse). Such language is visible all over Persius' satire. Thus Persius' ideas are often difficult to decipher, but the striking imagery in which they are packaged—imagery of disease, food, and slavery—make the reading (or listening) experience worth the work. We learn from the poet's ancient biography that his poems made him an instant sensation among the Roman literary elite, and that in particular the epic poet Lucan declared his own poems trifles next to Persius' (*Life of Persius* 48–49 and 20–22).

Persius also brilliantly evokes phrases and ideas from earlier writers, never just imitating them, but also taking them apart to examine and redeploy. The choliambic prologue mocks pretentious and derivative poetry; Persius finds his own way to use his models to say something new. He explicitly cites the examples of Lucilius and Horace in his programmatic *Satire* 1 as he begins his book of traditionally provocative, but unapologetically idiosyncratic, satiric poems (**1.1–12, 107–34**). Subsequently, the satirist begins to interrogate his audience (sometimes in the form of an internal addressee, such as Macrinus at **2.1**) on their grasp of reason. *Satire* 2 takes us into the private thoughts of people who present ambitious prayers to the gods, and dramatizes their foolishness and failure (**2.1–16, 31–51**). In *Satires* 3 and 4 Persius lectures people who are especially well-equipped to live according to reason, namely students of philosophy, but ones who have betrayed their training. In **Satire 5** he returns to his own case briefly and delivers an encomium to his tutor Cornutus (**5.21–51**) before demonstrating his acquired knowledge with a diatribe on the Stoic concept of true freedom. *Satire* 6 is the poet's valediction, delivered from a geographically remote retreat in the style of a letter to a friend, and seeming to announce the end of Persius' self-education (and of his guidance of others). The wisdom Persius treasures remains elusive to most readers, but he succeeds in framing life's problems in novel and provocative ways. There is nothing quite like the experience of reading Persius, in Latin or in English.

After Nero and more civil war (68–70 CE) came a new period of relative stability for the Empire under the rule of the Flavians (70–96 CE). The last Flavian emperor, Domitian, presided over (and actively sponsored) another explosion of poetic activity. The epigrammatist Martial and the epic poets Statius and Valerius Flaccus worked during Domitian's reign; so did a satiric poet named Turnus, whose poetry is lost except for a couple of lines. It was slightly later that Decimus Iunius Iuvenalis (**Juvenal**), a younger contemporary of Pliny and Tacitus, began to write his *Satires*. Juvenal is the satirist about whose life we know the least. If we may take a couple of fleeting remarks in his poems at face value, he had an ancestral home in Aquinum (in Latium; see map) and a residence in Rome. He has left us sixteen poems (the last incomplete, due to early damage to a key manuscript), and these are arranged in five books that were most likely composed and published separately. We can date the poems through internal historical references to the first three decades of the second century CE.

While he wrote during the age that Edward Gibbon later deemed the "most happy and prosperous" in human history (more specifically, during the reigns of the emperors Trajan and Hadrian), Juvenal finds plenty of fodder for satire and moral attack in Roman daily life. He is best known for the angry persona of his first two books of poems, where he vigorously attacks common vices such as greed

(**1.63–93** and **135–46**) and sexual debauchery (**6.60–102**). Juvenal explicitly encourages his readers to compare these over-the-top performances of indignation to grand epic and tragedy. In **Satire 1**, he surveys the deplorable state of contemporary Rome, and in the poems that follow he examines particular trends that distress him. Posing as a traditional Roman moralist championing the values of pre-Imperial Rome, Juvenal attacks sexually deviant men (*Satire* 2), the foreigners who are filling his city (3), the rich men who abjure their responsibility to poorer clients (3, 5), and Roman wives who wield non-traditional power (6). While his moral views are conservative, Juvenal does attack dissolute behavior among the Roman aristocracy and so occasionally comes across as a champion of ordinary folk (see, e.g., **3.190–231**). In a way this follows Horace's and Persius' convention of praising the humble life, but Juvenal is much more pointed in attacking social injustice when he wants to be.

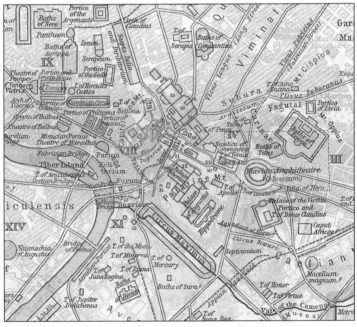

Fig. 1. Portion of William R. Shepherd's plan of Imperial Rome.

Nevertheless, Juvenal's political criticism often sounds like that of a proud blue-blooded Roman who wishes to see the upper classes recover their traditional ideals and roles, rather than that of a revolutionary. He turns his anger on the vain and tyrannical Domitian in *Satire* 4 (adhering to a vow made at the end of *Satire* 1 to restrict his personal attacks to dead people). This creates an interesting satiric counterpart to the accounts of the emperor's reign in Tacitus and Pliny, both champions (at least after the fact) of the senatorial opposition to Domitian. Tacitus in particular has a visible influence on the *Satires*; Juvenal incorporates considerably more historical material in his satire than his predecessors did, and we may even find glimpses of historical figures in his generic characters (for example, some of the "uppity wives" in **Satire 6** recall Tacitus' power-hungry Imperial women).

Juvenal's manipulation of his satiric persona also marks him as a product of his time. He claims to have been trained in literature and rhetoric (1.15–17), as all young men of means were in the first century CE, and this is an explicit signal to notice his many tricks: a range of distinct personae, clever literary and mythological parody, references to *au courant* philosophical schools and ideas, and witty *sententiae* (maxims) meant to sum up contemporary mores. Many of these devices emerge more prominently in the later poems, where the angry mode is replaced by more ironic and moderate masks. Juvenal has a stint posing as an ironic advisor (book 3) to struggling writers (*Satire* 7), immoral nobles (**8**), and even an embittered male prostitute (**9**). In describing the problems that plague these people's lives he shows mild irritation, not indignation, and he focuses on lacing his advice with allusions to philosophical dialogue and literary epistles. In the fourth and fifth books, Juvenal adopts a similarly distant persona, though there is variation depending on his subject-matter. There are poems with a clear focus and humanistic attitude reminiscent of Horatian diatribe, particularly *Satire* 10 on the folly of ambitious prayers, 11 on frugal dining, and **14** on parents' influence on their children. In other cases, the satirist shows a more restless and cynical take on human affairs. *Satire* 12 celebrates a friend's survival of shipwreck but culminates in a scathing attack on the false friendship of legacy-hunters (the theme of Horace's harsh **Satire 2.5**). Juvenal seems downright cruel and mocking in **Satire 13**, where he advises a wronged and angry friend to accept that humanity is hopelessly corrupt. The last two poems of book 5 are harsh enough to remind the reader of the early books: *Satire* 15 condemns an act of violent cannibalism in Egypt, and 16 bitterly compares the legal protections enjoyed by soldiers to the ordinary citizen's vulnerability. These last bouts of anti-foreign rhetoric and cries of lost rights echo the entertaining tirades in *Satires* 1 and 3. Overall, the later books have always remained somewhat on the margins in scholarship and in the classroom, but they contain some wonderfully entertaining and accessible material, such as the comparison of ancient and modern morals at **13.38–70** and the moral appeal to parents at **14.1–55**. *Satire* 10 is often the only later poem that students are encouraged to read, and its treatment of historical and mythological characters is brilliant, but there is also a treat to be found in the digression on theater and the emperor Nero at **8.183–99** and **215–30**.

Without a doubt, ten different instructors would choose ten different lists of selections for a volume like this one. In making my choices I have aimed at various goals: to trace the broad changes in satire from the Republic to the high Imperial period; to show each author's range of themes and strategies; to draw attention to the ways the authors imitate and modify one another's work; and occasionally to train the spotlight on a poem that might not otherwise make it onto course syllabi. But with space being limited, many passages that would make excellent class readings have not made it into the volume. Instructors are encouraged to bring in additional poems that would complement the ones represented here. Horace *Satires* 1.9 and 2.6 are reliable class favorites, and Persius 4 a workable challenge. Juvenal 10, while the ideas in it can be difficult to decipher, deserves its reputation as a masterpiece and is full of characters that students may know from studying ancient history and myth. There exist some serviceable older school texts of Horace and Juvenal, and

Bryn Mawr commentaries on Juvenal 6 (Richlin) and all of Persius
(Cowherd). Miller's anthology *Latin Verse Satire* (Routledge, 2005)
has several poems with commentary, as well as a selection of inter-
pretive essays. A few poems by each satirist, in Latin with facing
translation and notes, are included in Dominik and Wehrle's volume *Roman Verse Satire* (Bolchazy-Carducci, 1999). For classes with
more scholarly ambitions, there is Braund's commentary on Juvenal
book 1 (Cambridge, 1996), and soon Cambridge will also publish the
eagerly awaited commentaries on Horace *Satires* 1 and 2 by Gowers
and Freudenburg. Alternatively, instructors who wish to combine
satire with other genres will have many options, including config-
urations that use other recently published or forthcoming Readers
in this series. Verse satire would pair well with the comic drama of
Plautus or Terence, with Martial's *Epigrams*, with Apuleius' novel
Metamorphoses, or even with assorted sources on Roman women to
build a syllabus dealing with Roman social and domestic life.

∾ *Style and meter*

Reading Latin poetry typically requires students to be on the lookout
for poetic forms and devices, such as the frequent omission of forms
of *sum* (e.g., in perfect passive verbal constructions), the ending *-ere*
as an alternative to *-erunt* (not restricted to poetry, but seen there
often), and of course freedom with word order. Students can find
help on declensions of Greek names, which appear occasionally in
these selections, at GL 65 and B 47. Each satirist will present different challenges and yield different pleasures for the Latin student.
Many of Lucilius' fragments survived because they contained odd
vocabulary or forms and were therefore cited in late antique reference works, and these elements require some special commentary.
Lucilius generally uses what may be called a "luxuriant" style that
allows for a wide-ranging vocabulary, including Greek words, and
diction that varies from the colloquial to the grand (in imitation of
epic or tragedy). He does not hesitate to be repetitive in his phrasing
or use of sound effects. Horace calls Lucilius' verse "muddy" (*Satire*
1.4.11), and Horace's style of composition is indeed "more terse and

more pure" as Quintilian writes (*Education of the orator* 10.1.94). His creative ordering of words is not just a strategy for "making the meter work," as weary readers will sometimes speculate, but almost always helps Horace underscore the ideas he is conveying (e.g., through striking juxtaposition or delay of a word). A classic example is the so-called "golden line" that appears in much hexameter poetry, and which has a symmetrical structure: a verb in the center preceded by two adjectives and followed by two nouns in corresponding order. Such lines are easy for students to identify, and a good starting point for encouraging attention to composition in general. It will immediately become clear that Horace tends to be less repetitive than Lucilius in his phrasing, instead aiming for variation; this reflects careful work but the effect is a graceful simplicity and an illusion of real "chat."

Persius can rarely be called graceful. The notorious difficulty of his verse stems partly from his odd vocabulary and partly from his abrupt and elliptical way of walking through ideas and dialogue; students tend to struggle more with his ideas, less with his style of composition. But he does present, for example, some unusual constructions with infinitives (perfect for present, or completing the sense of adjectives) and internal accusatives. Finally, Juvenal steers away from Persius' brevity and revives, in some ways, the exuberance of Lucilius. One finds vulgar words juxtaposed with the grand vocabulary suited to epic and tragedy. But Juvenal's compositional style is purposeful and ingenious, even including the occasional "golden line." Some particularly Juvenalian devices that are well represented in these selections are diminutive forms, rhetorical questions, anaphora (repetition of a word at the beginning of successive clauses), and synecdoche (or "part for the whole"). With practice, students will come to anticipate his rhythm in building momentum toward hyperbolic rhetorical climaxes or deflating witticisms.

All the selections in this book are in dactylic hexameter, the meter chosen by Lucilius for his later satires and by all three of his successors in the genre. This was the traditional meter of heroic and national epic in both Greek and Latin, and so the genre of "chat," miscellany, and diatribe was ironically linked to the grandest poetic genre of Greco-Roman antiquity. The authors of satire manage to make the hexameter seem appropriate for their whole range of modes: mundane commentary on human affairs, intense moralistic attacks, and lively parodies. As with any Latin poetry, students will benefit from reading the passages aloud, not just to clarify the occasional ambiguous word-ending, but to appreciate the authors' play with sound and rhythm. The structure, rules, and typical patterns of the dactylic hexameter are outlined fully in B 362–68 and GL 702–6 and 783–84.

∾ *Suggested Further Reading* (all in English)
Introduction to the satiric genre and relevant scholarship

Hooley, D. *Roman Satire*. Malden, MA: Blackwell Publishers, 2007. (An up-to-date introduction to the genre, its authors, and its ancient contexts.)

Books and collections of essays on satire

Anderson, W. *Essays on Roman Satire*. Princeton: Princeton University Press, 1982. (Collected essays on the rhetoric and themes of satire, including separate analyses of the individual poets.)

Braund, S., ed. *Satire and Society in Ancient Rome*. Exeter: University of Exeter Press, 1989. (Essays by various scholars on key social themes of satire.)

Freudenburg, K. *Satires of Rome: Threatening Poses from Lucilius to Juvenal*. Cambridge: Cambridge University Press, 2001. (A study of satire's literary and political entanglements after Lucilius.)

Freudenburg, K., ed. *Cambridge Companion to Roman Satire*. Cambridge: Cambridge University Press, 2005. (Essays by various scholars on satire's literary strategies and political relevance.)

Gowers, E. *The Loaded Table: Representations of Food in Roman Literature*. Oxford: Oxford University Press, 1993. (An analysis of the food theme in Roman literature, including satire.)

Henderson, J. *Writing Down Rome: Satire, Comedy, and Other Of-fences in Latin Poetry.* Oxford: Oxford University Press, 1999. (Collected essays on Roman comic genres, including satire, and their relation to Roman culture and identity.)

Keane, C. *Figuring Genre in Roman Satire.* Oxford: Oxford University Press, 2006. (A study of satire's range of social agendas and methods of self-reference.)

Plaza, M. *The Function of Humour in Roman Verse Satire.* Oxford: Oxford University Press, 2006. (An analysis of satire's strategies of humor.)

Books on the individual satirists with philological and theoretical approaches

Braund. S. *Beyond Anger: A Study of Juvenal's Third Book of Satires.* Cambridge: Cambridge University Press, 1988. (On Juvenal's rhetorical persona in *Satires* 7–9, in the context of his rhetorical development as a whole.)

Freudenburg, K. *The Walking Muse: Horace on the Theory of Satire.* Princeton: Princeton University Press, 1993. (Analysis of Horace's diatribe style and ironic techniques, particularly in the early *Satires* of book 1.)

Hooley, D. *The Knotted Thong: Structures of Mimesis in Persius.* Ann Arbor: University of Michigan Press, 1997. (Analysis of Persius' literary allusions and satiric aims.)

Jones, F. *Juvenal and the Satiric Genre.* London: Duckworth Publishers, 2007. (On Juvenal's positioning of satire in Roman literary tradition.)

Schlegel, C. *Satire and the Threat of Speech in Horace* Satires *I.* Madison: University of Wisconsin Press, 2005. (On Horace's self-portrait in *Satires* book 1 and his representation of the benefits and problems of his genre.)

Latin text

In this text, consonantal *u* is printed as *v* throughout. Only proper nouns and related adjectives are capitalized. In addition, I make the following small changes to the editions listed in the Preface, with explanation in the notes where necessary:

Horace 1.4.122: the semicolon after **hoc** is changed to a comma

Horace 2.5.32: the comma is moved to line 33 after the parentheses

Juvenal 6.65: here printed without brackets

Juvenal 14.1: the spurious line often printed after this ("1A" in Clausen's text) is omitted

❧ *Lucilius*

Scenes from a gladiatorial match, *Satires*, fragments 172–75, 176–81, 185

Aeserninus fuit Flaccorum munere quidam

Samnis, spurcus homo, vita illa dignus locoque.

cum Pacideiano conponitur, optimus multo

175 post homines natos gladiator qui fuit unus.

'occidam illum equidem et vincam, si id quaeritis,' inquit.

'verum illud credo fore: in os prius accipiam ipse,

quam gladium in stomacho surdi ac pulmonibus sisto.

odi hominem, iratus pugno, nec longius quicquam

180   nobis, quam dextrae gladium dum accommodet alter;
       usque adeo studio atque odio illius ecferor ira.'

185   haerebat mucro gladiumque in pectore totum.

Human superstition, *Satires*, fragments 524–29

       terriculas Lamias, Fauni quas Pompiliique
525   instituere Numae, tremit has hic omnia ponit.
       ut pueri infantes credunt signa omnia aena
       vivere et esse homines, sic isti somnia ficta
       vera putant, credunt signis cor inesse in aenis.
       pergula pictorum, veri nil, omnia ficta.

The Roman rat-race, *Satires*, fragments 1145–51

1145 nunc vero a mani ad noctem festo atque profesto
       totus item pariterque die populusque patresque
       iactare indu foro se omnes, decedere nusquam;
       uni se atque eidem studio omnes dedere et arti—
       verba dare ut caute possint, pugnare dolose,
1150 blanditia certare, bonum simulare virum se,
       insidias facere ut si hostes sint omnibus omnes.

A definition of virtue, *Satires*, fragments 1196–1208

       virtus, Albine, est pretium persolvere verum
       quis in versamur quis vivimus rebus potesse;
       virtus est homini scire id quod quaeque habeat res;
       virtus scire homini rectum utile quid sit honestum,
1200 quae bona quae mala item, quid inutile turpe inhonestum;

virtus quaerendae finem re scire modumque;

virtus divitiis pretium persolvere posse;

virtus id dare quod re ipsa debetur honori,

hostem esse atque inimicum hominum morumque malorum

1205　contra defensorem hominum morumque bonorum,

hos magni facere, his bene velle, his vivere amicum,

commoda praeterea patriai prima putare,

deinde parentum, tertia iam postremaque nostra.

∾ *Horace*

Greed and its manifestations, *Satire* 1.1.41–79

quid iuvat inmensum te argenti pondus et auri

furtim defossa timidum deponere terra?

'quod si comminuas vilem redigatur ad assem.'

at ni id fit, quid habet pulchri constructus acervus?

45　milia frumenti tua triverit area centum,

non tuus hoc capiet venter plus ac meus: ut si

reticulum panis venalis inter onusto

forte vehas umero, nihilo plus accipias quam
qui nil portarit. vel dic quid referat intra

50　naturae finis viventi, iugera centum an

mille aret? 'at suave est ex magno tollere acervo.'

dum ex parvo nobis tantundem haurire relinquas,

cur tua plus laudes cumeris granaria nostris?

ut tibi si sit opus liquidi non amplius urna

55　vel cyatho, et dicas 'magno de flumine mallem

quam ex hoc fonticulo tantundem sumere.' eo fit

plenior ut si quos delectet copia iusto,

cum ripa simul avulsos ferat Aufidus acer.
at qui tantuli eget quanto est opus, is neque limo
60   turbatam haurit aquam, neque vitam amittit in undis.
at bona pars hominum decepta cupidine falso
'nil satis est' inquit, 'quia tanti quantum habeas sis.'
quid facias illi? iubeas miserum esse, libenter
quatenus id facit: ut quidam memoratur Athenis
65   sordidus ac dives, populi contemnere voces
sic solitus: 'populus me sibilat; at mihi plaudo
ipse domi, simul ac nummos contemplor in arca.'
Tantalus a labris sitiens fugientia captat
flumina—quid rides? mutato nomine de te
70   fabula narratur; congestis undique saccis
indormis inhians et tamquam parcere sacris
cogeris aut pictis tamquam gaudere tabellis.
nescis quo valeat nummus, quem praebeat usum?
panis ematur, holus, vini sextarius, adde
75   quis humana sibi doleat natura negatis.
an vigilare metu exanimem, noctesque diesque
formidare malos fures, incendia, servos,
ne te compilent fugientes, hoc iuvat? horum
semper ego optarim pauperrimus esse bonorum.

Horace defends his satire, *Satire* 1.4.103–43

                                        liberius si
dixero quid, si forte iocosius, hoc mihi iuris
105   cum venia dabis: insuevit pater optimus hoc me,
ut fugerem exemplis vitiorum quaeque notando.

cum me hortaretur, parce, frugaliter, atque
viverem uti contentus eo quod mi ipse parasset,
'nonne vides Albi ut male vivat filius, utque
110   Baius inops? magnum documentum ne patriam rem
perdere quis velit': a turpi meretricis amore
cum deterreret, 'Scetani dissimilis sis':
ne sequerer moechas concessa cum venere uti
possem, 'deprensi non bella est fama Treboni'
115   aiebat: 'sapiens, vitatu quidque petitu
sit melius, causas reddet tibi: mi satis est si
traditum ab antiquis morem servare tuamque,
dum custodis eges, vitam famamque tueri
incolumem possum; simul ac duraverit aetas
120   membra animumque tuum, nabis sine cortice.' Sic me
formabat puerum dictis; et sive iubebat
ut facerem quid, 'habes auctorem quo facias hoc',
unum ex iudicibus selectis obiciebat;
sive vetabat, 'an hoc inhonestum et inutile factu
125   necne sit addubites, flagret rumore malo cum
hic atque ille?' avidos vicinum funus ut aegros
exanimat mortisque metu sibi parcere cogit,
sic teneros animos aliena opprobria saepe
absterrent vitiis. ex hoc ego sanus ab illis,
130   perniciem quaecumque ferunt, mediocribus et quis
ignoscas vitiis teneor. fortassis et istinc
largiter abstulerit longa aetas, liber amicus,
consilium proprium, neque enim, cum lectulus aut me
porticus excepit, desum mihi: 'rectius hoc est:

135 hoc faciens vivam melius: sic dulcis amicis
     occurram: hoc quidam non belle; numquid ego illi
     inprudens olim faciam simile?' haec ego mecum
     compressis agito labris; ubi quid datur oti
     illudo chartis. hoc est mediocribus illis
140 ex vitiis unum; cui si concedere nolis,
     multa poetarum veniat manus auxilio quae
     sit mihi (nam multo plures sumus), ac veluti te
     Iudaei cogemus in hanc concedere turbam.

How to hunt legacies, *Satire* 2.5.23–50

     'dixi equidem et dico: captes astutus ubique
     testamenta senum, neu, si vafer unus et alter
25   insidiatorem praeroso fugerit hamo,
     aut spem deponas aut artem illusus omittas.
     magna minorve foro si res certabitur olim,
     vivet uter locuples sine gnatis, improbus, ultro
     qui meliorem audax vocet in ius, illius esto
30   defensor; fama civem causaque priorem
     sperne, domi si gnatus erit fecundave coniunx.
     'Quinte,' puta, aut 'Publi' (gaudent praenomine molles
     auriculae), 'tibi me virtus tua fecit amicum;
     ius anceps novi, causas defendere possum;
35   eripiet quivis oculos citius mihi quam te
     contemptum cassa nuce pauperet; haec mea cura est,
     ne quid tu perdas neu sis iocus.' ire domum atque
     pelliculam curare iube; fi cognitor ipse,
     persta atque obdura, seu rubra Canicula findet

40   infantis statuas, seu pingui tentus omaso
      Furius hibernas cana nive conspuet Alpis.
      'nonne vides,' aliquis cubito stantem prope tangens
      inquiet, 'ut patiens, ut amicis aptus, ut acer?'
      plures adnabunt thynni et cetaria crescent.
45   si cui praeterea validus male filius in re
      praeclara sublatus aletur, ne manifestum
      caelibis obsequium nudet te, leniter in spem
      adrepe officiosus, ut et scribare secundus
      heres et, si quis casus puerum egerit Orco,
50   in vacuum venias: perraro haec alea fallit.

The satirist in the hot seat, *Satire* 2.7.21–71

      non dices hodie, quorsum haec tam putida tendant,
      furcifer? 'ad te, inquam.' quo pacto, pessime? 'laudas
      fortunam et mores antiquae plebis, et idem
      si quis ad illa deus subito te agat, usque recuses,
25   aut quia non sentis quod clamas rectius esse,
      aut quia non firmus rectum defendis, et haeres
      nequiquam caeno cupiens evellere plantam.
      Romae rus optas, absentem rusticus urbem
      tollis ad astra levis. si nusquam es forte vocatus
30   ad cenam laudas securum holus ac, velut usquam
      vinctus eas, ita te felicem dicis amasque
      quod nusquam tibi sit potandum. iusserit ad se
      Maecenas serum sub lumina prima venire
      convivam: 'nemon oleum feret ocius? ecquis
35   audit?' cum magno blateras clamore fugisque.

Mulvius et scurrae tibi non referenda precati

discedunt. 'etenim fateor me' dixerit ille

'duci ventre levem, nasum nidore supinor,

imbecillus, iners, si quid vis, adde, popino.

40 tu cum sis quod ego et fortassis nequior, ultro

insectere velut melior verbisque decoris

obvolvas vitium?' quid, si me stultior ipso

quingentis empto drachmis deprenderis? aufer

me vultu terrere; manum stomachumque teneto,

45 dum quae Crispini docuit me ianitor edo.

te coniunx aliena capit, meretricula Davum:

peccat uter nostrum cruce dignius? acris ubi me

natura intendit, sub clara nuda lucerna

quaecumque excepit turgentis verbera caudae,

50 clunibus aut agitavit equum lasciva supinum,

dimittit neque famosum neque sollicitum ne

ditior aut formae melioris meiat eodem.

tu cum proiectis insignibus, anulo equestri

Romanoque habitu, prodis ex iudice Dama

55 turpis, odoratum caput obscurante lacerna,

non es quod simulas? metuens induceris atque

altercante libidinibus tremis ossa pavore.

quid refert, uri virgis, ferroque necari

auctoratus eas, an turpi clausus in arca,

60 quo te demisit peccati conscia erilis,

contractum genibus tangas caput? estne marito

matronae peccantis in ambo iusta potestas?

in corruptorem vel iustior. illa tamen se

non habitu mutatve loco, peccatve superne.

65 cum te formidet mulier neque credat amanti,

ibis sub furcam prudens, dominoque furenti

committes rem omnem et vitam et cum corpore famam.

evasti: credo, metues doctusque cavebis:

quaeres quando iterum paveas iterumque perire

70 possis, o totiens servus! quae belua ruptis,

cum semel effugit, reddit se prava catenis?

The satirist in the hot seat (continued), *Satire* 2.7.111–18

adde quod idem

non horam tecum esse potes, non otia recte

ponere, teque ipsum vitas fugitivus et erro,

iam vino quaerens, iam somno fallere curam:

115 frustra; nam comes atra premit sequiturque fugacem.'

unde mihi lapidem? 'quorsum est opus?' unde sagittas?

'aut insanit homo aut versus facit.' ocius hinc te

ni rapis, accedes opera agro nona Sabino.

∾ *Persius*

A self-sufficient satirist, *Satire* 1.1–12

o curas hominum! o quantum est in rebus inane!

'quis leget haec?' min tu istud ais? nemo hercule. 'nemo?'

vel duo vel nemo. 'turpe et miserabile.' quare?

ne mihi Polydamas et Troiades Labeonem

5 praetulerint? nugae. non, si quid turbida Roma

elevet, accedas examenve inprobum in illa

castiges trutina nec te quaesiveris extra.

nam Romae quis non—a, si fas dicere—sed fas
tum cum ad canitiem et nostrum istud vivere triste
10   aspexi ac nucibus facimus quaecumque relictis,
cum sapimus patruos. tunc tunc—ignoscite (nolo,
quid faciam?) sed sum petulanti splene—cachinno.

A self-sufficient satirist (continued), *Satire* 1.107–34

'sed quid opus teneras mordaci radere vero
auriculas? vide sis ne maiorum tibi forte
limina frigescant: sonat hic de nare canina
110   littera.' per me equidem sint omnia protinus alba;
nil moror. euge omnes, omnes bene, mirae eritis res.
hoc iuvat? 'hic' inquis 'veto quisquam faxit oletum.'
pinge duos anguis: 'pueri, sacer est locus, extra
meiite.' discedo. secuit Lucilius urbem,
115   te Lupe, te Muci, et genuinum fregit in illis.
omne vafer vitium ridenti Flaccus amico
tangit et admissus circum praecordia ludit,
callidus excusso populum suspendere naso.
me muttire nefas? nec clam? nec cum scrobe? nusquam?
120   hic tamen infodiam. vidi, vidi ipse, libelle:
auriculas asini quis non habet? hoc ego opertum,
hoc ridere meum, tam nil, nulla tibi vendo
Iliade. audaci quicumque adflate Cratino
iratum Eupolidem praegrandi cum sene palles,
125   aspice et haec, si forte aliquid decoctius audis.
inde vaporata lector mihi ferveat aure,

non hic qui in crepidas Graiorum ludere gestit
sordidus et lusco qui possit dicere 'lusce,'
sese aliquem credens Italo quod honore supinus
130 fregerit heminas Arreti aedilis iniquas,
nec qui abaco numeros et secto in pulvere metas
scit risisse vafer, multum gaudere paratus
si cynico barbam petulans nonaria vellat.
his mane edictum, post prandia Callirhoen do.

Foolish prayers, *Satire* 2.1–16

hunc, Macrine, diem numera meliore lapillo,
qui tibi labentis apponit candidus annos.
funde merum genio. non tu prece poscis emaci
quae nisi seductis nequeas committere divis;
5 at bona pars procerum tacita libabit acerra.
haut cuivis promptum est murmurque humilisque susurros
tollere de templis et aperto vivere voto.
'mens bona, fama, fides', haec clare et ut audiat hospes;
illa sibi introrsum et sub lingua murmurat: 'o si
10 ebulliat patruus, praeclarum funus!' et 'o si
sub rastro crepet argenti mihi seria dextro
Hercule! pupillumve utinam, quem proximus heres
inpello, expungam; nam et est scabiosus et acri
bile tumet. Nerio iam tertia conditur uxor.'
15 haec sancte ut poscas, Tiberino in gurgite mergis
mane caput bis terque et noctem flumine purgas.

Foolish prayers (continued), *Satire* 2.31–51

ecce avia aut metuens divum matertera cunis
exemit puerum frontemque atque uda labella
infami digito et lustralibus ante salivis
expiat, urentis oculos inhibere perita;

35 tunc manibus quatit et spem macram supplice voto
nunc Licini in campos, nunc Crassi mittit in aedis:
'hunc optet generum rex et regina, puellae
hunc rapiant; quidquid calcaverit hic, rosa fiat.'
ast ego nutrici non mando vota. negato,

40 Iuppiter, haec illi, quamvis te albata rogarit.
    poscis opem nervis corpusque fidele senectae.
esto age. sed grandes patinae tuccetaque crassa
adnuere his superos vetuere Iovemque morantur.
rem struere exoptas caeso bove Mercuriumque

45 arcessis fibra: 'da fortunare Penatis,
da pecus et gregibus fetum.' quo, pessime, pacto,
tot tibi cum in flamma iunicum omenta liquescant?
et tamen hic extis et opimo vincere ferto
intendit: 'iam crescit ager, iam crescit ovile,

50 iam dabitur, iam iam'—donec deceptus et exspes
nequiquam fundo suspiret nummus in imo.

The satirist's philosophical and ethical roots, *Satire* 5.21–51

secrete loquimur. tibi nunc hortante Camena
excutienda damus praecordia, quantaque nostrae
pars tua sit, Cornute, animae, tibi, dulcis amice,

ostendisse iuvat. pulsa, dinoscere cautus

25 quid solidum crepet et pictae tectoria linguae.

hic ego centenas ausim deposcere fauces,

ut quantum mihi te sinuoso in pectore fixi

voce traham pura, totumque hoc verba resignent

quod latet arcana non enarrabile fibra.

30   cum primum pavido custos mihi purpura cessit

bullaque subcinctis Laribus donata pependit,

cum blandi comites totaque inpune Subura

permisit sparsisse oculos iam candidus umbo,

cumque iter ambiguum est et vitae nescius error

35 diducit trepidas ramosa in compita mentes,

me tibi supposui. teneros tu suscipis annos

Socratico, Cornute, sinu. tum fallere sollers

adposita intortos extendit regula mores

et premitur ratione animus vincique laborat

40 artificemque tuo ducit sub pollice voltum.

tecum etenim longos memini consumere soles

et tecum primas epulis decerpere noctes.

unum opus et requiem pariter disponimus ambo

atque verecunda laxamus seria mensa.

45 non equidem hoc dubites, amborum foedere certo

consentire dies et ab uno sidere duci.

nostra vel aequali suspendit tempora Libra

Parca tenax veri, seu nata fidelibus hora

dividit in Geminos concordia fata duorum

50 Saturnumque gravem nostro Iove frangimus una,

nescio quod certe est quod me tibi temperat astrum.

∾ Juvenal

Identifying a crisis, *Satire* 1.63–93

nonne libet medio ceras inplere capaces

quadrivio, cum iam sexta cervice feratur

65 hinc atque inde patens ac nuda paene cathedra

et multum referens de Maecenate supino

signator falsi, qui se lautum atque beatum

exiguis tabulis et gemma fecerit uda?

occurrit matrona potens, quae molle Calenum

70 porrectura viro miscet sitiente rubetam

instituitque rudes melior Lucusta propinquas

per famam et populum nigros efferre maritos.

aude aliquid brevibus Gyaris et carcere dignum,

si vis esse aliquid. probitas laudatur et alget;

75 criminibus debent hortos, praetoria, mensas,

argentum vetus et stantem extra pocula caprum.

quem patitur dormire nurus corruptor avarae,

quem sponsae turpes et praetextatus adulter?

si natura negat, facit indignatio versum

80 qualemcumque potest, quales ego vel Cluvienus.

    ex quo Deucalion nimbis tollentibus aequor

navigio montem ascendit sortesque poposcit

paulatimque anima caluerunt mollia saxa

et maribus nudas ostendit Pyrrha puellas,

85 quidquid agunt homines, votum, timor, ira, voluptas,

gaudia, discursus, nostri farrago libelli est.

et quando uberior vitiorum copia? quando

maior avaritiae patuit sinus? alea quando

hos animos? neque enim loculis comitantibus itur
90   ad casum tabulae, posita sed luditur arca.
proelia quanta illic dispensatore videbis
armigero! simplexne furor sestertia centum
perdere et horrenti tunicam non reddere servo?

Identifying a crisis (continued), *Satire* 1.135–46

135   optima silvarum interea pelagique vorabit
rex horum vacuisque toris tantum ipse iacebit.
nam de tot pulchris et latis orbibus et tam
antiquis una comedunt patrimonia mensa.
nullus iam parasitus erit. sed quis ferat istas
140   luxuriae sordes? quanta est gula quae sibi totos
ponit apros, animal propter convivia natum!
poena tamen praesens, cum tu deponis amictus
turgidus et crudum pavonem in balnea portas.
hinc subitae mortes atque intestata senectus.
145   it nova nec tristis per cunctas fabula cenas;
ducitur iratis plaudendum funus amicis.

Trials of the urban poor, *Satire* 3.190–231

190   quis timet aut timuit gelida Praeneste ruinam
aut positis nemorosa inter iuga Volsiniis aut
simplicibus Gabiis aut proni Tiburis arce?
nos urbem colimus tenui tibicine fultam
magna parte sui; nam sic labentibus obstat
195   vilicus et, veteris rimae cum texit hiatum,
securos pendente iubet dormire ruina.

vivendum est illic, ubi nulla incendia, nulli

nocte metus. iam poscit aquam, iam frivola transfert

Ucalegon, tabulata tibi iam tertia fumant:

200 tu nescis; nam si gradibus trepidatur ab imis,

ultimus ardebit quem tegula sola tuetur

a pluvia, molles ubi reddunt ova columbae.

lectus erat Cordo Procula minor, urceoli sex

ornamentum abaci, nec non et parvulus infra

205 cantharus et recubans sub eodem marmore Chiron,

iamque vetus Graecos servabat cista libellos

et divina opici rodebant carmina mures.

nil habuit Cordus, quis enim negat? et tamen illud

perdidit infelix totum nihil. ultimus autem

210 aerumnae cumulus, quod nudum et frusta rogantem

nemo cibo, nemo hospitio tectoque iuvabit.

si magna Asturici cecidit domus, horrida mater,

pullati proceres, differt vadimonia praetor.

tum gemimus casus urbis, tunc odimus ignem.

215 ardet adhuc, et iam accurrit qui marmora donet,

conferat inpensas; hic nuda et candida signa,

hic aliquid praeclarum Euphranoris et Polycliti,

haec Asianorum vetera ornamenta deorum,

hic libros dabit et forulos mediamque Minervam,

220 hic modium argenti. meliora ac plura reponit

Persicus orborum lautissimus et merito iam

suspectus tamquam ipse suas incenderit aedes.

si potes avelli circensibus, optima Sorae

aut Fabrateriae domus aut Frusinone paratur

225 quanti nunc tenebras unum conducis in annum.

hortulus hic puteusque brevis nec reste movendus

in tenuis plantas facili diffunditur haustu.

vive bidentis amans et culti vilicus horti

unde epulum possis centum dare Pythagoreis.

230 est aliquid, quocumque loco, quocumque recessu,

unius sese dominum fecisse lacertae.

Unchaste women on display, *Satire* 6.60–102

60 porticibusne tibi monstratur femina voto

digna tuo? cuneis an habent spectacula totis

quod securus ames quodque inde excerpere possis?

chironomon Ledam molli saltante Bathyllo

Tuccia vesicae non imperat, Apula gannit,

65 sicut in amplexu, subito et miserabile longum.

attendit Thymele: Thymele tunc rustica discit.

ast aliae, quotiens aulaea recondita cessant,

et vacuo clusoque sonant fora sola theatro,

atque a plebeis longe Megalesia, tristes

70 personam thyrsumque tenent et subligar Acci.

Urbicus exodio risum movet Atellanae

gestibus Autonoes, hunc diligit Aelia pauper.

solvitur his magno comoedi fibula, sunt quae

Chrysogonum cantare vetent, Hispulla tragoedo

75 gaudet: an expectas ut Quintilianus ametur?

accipis uxorem de qua citharoedus Echion

aut Glaphyrus fiat pater Ambrosiusque choraules.

longa per angustos figamus pulpita vicos,

ornentur postes et grandi ianua lauro,

80   ut testudineo tibi, Lentule, conopeo

nobilis Euryalum murmillonem exprimat infans.

nupta senatori comitata est Eppia ludum

ad Pharon et Nilum famosaque moenia Lagi

prodigia et mores urbis damnante Canopo.

85   inmemor illa domus et coniugis atque sororis

nil patriae indulsit, plorantisque improba natos

utque magis stupeas ludos Paridemque reliquit.

sed quamquam in magnis opibus plumaque paterna

et segmentatis dormisset parvula cunis,

90   contempsit pelagus; famam contempserat olim,

cuius apud molles minima est iactura cathedras.

Tyrrhenos igitur fluctus lateque sonantem

pertulit Ionium constanti pectore, quamvis

mutandum totiens esset mare. iusta pericli

95   si ratio est et honesta, timent pavidoque gelantur

pectore nec tremulis possunt insistere plantis:

fortem animum praestant rebus quas turpiter audent.

si iubeat coniunx, durum est conscendere navem,

tunc sentina gravis, tunc summus vertitur aer:

100   quae moechum sequitur, stomacho valet. illa maritum

convomit, haec inter nautas et prandet et errat

per puppem et duros gaudet tractare rudentis.

The scandal of performing nobles, *Satire* 8.183–99

quid si numquam adeo foedis adeoque pudendis

utimur exemplis, ut non peiora supersint?

185 consumptis opibus vocem, Damasippe, locasti

sipario, clamosum ageres ut Phasma Catulli.

Laureolum velox etiam bene Lentulus egit,

iudice me dignus vera cruce. nec tamen ipsi

ignoscas populo; populi frons durior huius,

190 qui sedet et spectat triscurria patriciorum,

planipedes audit Fabios, ridere potest qui

Mamercorum alapas. quanti sua funera vendant

quid refert? vendunt nullo cogente Nerone,

nec dubitant celsi praetoris vendere ludis.

195 finge tamen gladios inde atque hinc pulpita poni,

quid satius? mortem sic quisquam exhorruit, ut sit

zelotypus Thymeles, stupidi collega Corinthi?

res haut mira tamen citharoedo principe mimus

nobilis.

The scandal of performing nobles (continued), *Satire* 8.215–30

215 par Agamemnonidae crimen, sed causa facit rem

dissimilem. quippe ille deis auctoribus ultor

patris erat caesi media inter pocula, sed nec

Electrae iugulo se polluit aut Spartani

sanguine coniugii, nullis aconita propinquis

220 miscuit, in scena numquam cantavit Orestes,

Troica non scripsit. quid enim Verginius armis

      debuit ulcisci magis aut cum Vindice Galba,
      quod Nero tam saeva crudaque tyrannide fecit?
      haec opera atque hae sunt generosi principis artes,
225 gaudentis foedo peregrina ad pulpita cantu
      prostitui Graiaeque apium meruisse coronae.
      maiorum effigies habeant insignia vocis,
      ante pedes Domiti longum tu pone Thyestae
      syrma vel Antigones seu personam Melanippes,
230 et de marmoreo citharam suspende colosso.

The good old days, *Satire* 13.38–70

      quondam hoc indigenae vivebant more, priusquam
      sumeret agrestem posito diademate falcem
40   Saturnus fugiens, tunc cum virguncula Iuno
      et privatus adhuc Idaeis Iuppiter antris;
      nulla super nubes convivia caelicolarum
      nec puer Iliacus formonsa nec Herculis uxor
      ad cyathos et iam siccato nectare tergens
45   bracchia Volcanus Liparaea nigra taberna;
      prandebat sibi quisque deus nec turba deorum
      talis ut est hodie, contentaque sidera paucis
      numinibus miserum urguebant Atlanta minori
      pondere; nondum imi sortitus triste profundi
50   imperium Sicula torvos cum coniuge Pluton,
      nec rota nec Furiae nec saxum aut volturis atri
      poena, sed infernis hilares sine regibus umbrae.
      inprobitas illo fuit admirabilis aevo,
      credebant quo grande nefas et morte piandum

55 si iuvenis vetulo non adsurrexerat et si
    barbato cuicumque puer, licet ipse videret
    plura domi fraga et maiores glandis acervos;
    tam venerabile erat praecedere quattuor annis
    primaque par adeo sacrae lanugo senectae.
60 nunc si depositum non infitietur amicus,
    si reddat veterem cum tota aerugine follem,
    prodigiosa fides et Tuscis digna libellis
    quaeque coronata lustrari debeat agna.
    egregium sanctumque virum si cerno, bimembri
65 hoc monstrum puero et miranti sub aratro
    piscibus inventis et fetae comparo mulae,
    sollicitus, tamquam lapides effuderit imber
    examenque apium longa consederit uva
    culmine delubri, tamquam in mare fluxerit amnis
70 gurgitibus miris et lactis vertice torrens.

Parents who teach vice, *Satire* 14.1–55

    plurima sunt, Fuscine, et fama digna sinistra
    et nitidis maculam haesuram figentia rebus,
    quae monstrant ipsi pueris traduntque parentes.
    si damnosa senem iuvat alea, ludit et heres
5   bullatus parvoque eadem movet arma fritillo.
    nec melius de se cuiquam sperare propinquo
    concedet iuvenis, qui radere tubera terrae,
    boletum condire et eodem iure natantis
    mergere ficedulas didicit nebulone parente
10 et cana monstrante gula. cum septimus annus

transierit puerum, nondum omni dente renato,
barbatos licet admoveas mille inde magistros,
hinc totidem, cupiet lauto cenare paratu
semper et a magna non degenerare culina.
15 mitem animum et mores modicis erroribus aequos
praecipit atque animas servorum et corpora nostra
materia constare putat paribusque elementis,
an saevire docet Rutilus, qui gaudet acerbo
plagarum strepitu et nullam Sirena flagellis
20 conparat, Antiphates trepidi laris ac Polyphemus,
tunc felix, quotiens aliquis tortore vocato
uritur ardenti duo propter lintea ferro?
quid suadet iuveni laetus stridore catenae,
quem mire adficiunt inscripta, ergastula, carcer?
25 rusticus expectas ut non sit adultera Largae
filia, quae numquam maternos dicere moechos
tam cito nec tanto poterit contexere cursu
ut non ter deciens respiret? conscia matri
virgo fuit, ceras nunc hac dictante pusillas
30 implet et ad moechum dat eisdem ferre cinaedis.
sic natura iubet: velocius et citius nos
corrumpunt vitiorum exempla domestica, magnis
cum subeant animos auctoribus. unus et alter
forsitan haec spernant iuvenes, quibus arte benigna
35 et meliore luto finxit praecordia Titan,
sed reliquos fugienda patrum vestigia ducunt
et monstrata diu veteris trahit orbita culpae.
abstineas igitur damnandis. huius enim vel

una potens ratio est, ne crimina nostra sequantur

40   ex nobis geniti, quoniam dociles imitandis

turpibus ac pravis omnes sumus, et Catilinam

quocumque in populo videas, quocumque sub axe,

sed nec Brutus erit Bruti nec avunculus usquam.

nil dictu foedum visuque haec limina tangat

45   intra quae pater est. procul, a procul inde puellae

lenonum et cantus pernoctantis parasiti.

maxima debetur puero reverentia, si quid

turpe paras, nec tu pueri contempseris annos,

sed peccaturo obstet tibi filius infans.

50   nam si quid dignum censoris fecerit ira

quandoque et similem tibi se non corpore tantum

nec vultu dederit, morum quoque filius et qui

omnia deterius tua per vestigia peccet,

corripies nimirum et castigabis acerbo

55   clamore ac post haec tabulas mutare parabis.

Fig. 2. Map: Locations in Roman Italy mentioned in the texts and notes

Commentary

All references in **bold** refer to passages in the volume.

∾ *Scenes from a gladiatorial match,* Lucilius, *Satires,* fragments 172–75, 176–81, and 185

These three fragments come to us from different sources; modern scholars assembling Lucilius' fragments recognized that they belonged together. The satirist introduces two gladiatorial combatants in a mock-epic fashion. One of them makes a lively preliminary speech (we possess this fragment because Cicero quotes it to illustrate violent rage at *Tusculan Disputations* 4.48). We may have an image of the battle's climax in line 185, although some editors believe this comes from a different part of Lucilius' work.

172   **Aeserninus . . . quidam** the first word is either a name or an adj. indicating the man's home Aesernia, a Samnite town (see note on 173). Here and in much other archaic Latin poetry (see, e.g., *dignus* in 173), the end syllable *-us* is pronounced short before a consonant.

     Flaccorum the family that sponsored the show (*munus*)

     munere abl. of time

173   **Samnis** the Samnites were a people who inhabited the central southern Apennine mountains (see map: "Samnium"), but gladiators who wore the heavy armor of that people were also known as "Samnites"

     spurcus this usually means "unclean," but Nonius, the grammarian who cites the fragment, claims that it means "cruel" here. He may have based his interpretation on parallel instances in texts that were later lost.

vita illa . . . locoque *illa* applies to both nouns

174 **cum** the prep., underscoring the prefix of the verb

optimus follows *qui fuit* in 175. Epic poets make similar grand claims about their heroes; Lucilius is showing his talent for parody.

multo abl. of degree of difference

175 **post homines natos** "since people were (first) born," "since the dawn of humanity"

unus "alone," "the single"

Fig. 3. Graffito of victorious gladiator carrying palm branch (Pompeii, Imperial period).

176–81 **occidam . . . ira** Pacideianus speaks.

176–77 **occidam . . . vincam . . . accipiam** all fut. indicative

177 **illud** the acc. subject of *fore*

os supply *meum*; also supply an object for *accipiam*—e.g., "blows."

prius linked with *quam* in 178

178 **gladium** appears in its usual masculine form here and in 180

surdi understand this to modify Pacideianus' opponent, and take as a substantive. The text is slightly corrupt at this word, but the reading printed here (Warmington's) is easiest to decipher.

179–80 **nec longius . . . dum accomodet alter** "nor (will this fight last) any longer for us, than the time it takes the other guy to . . ."

179 **quicquam** adverbial: "at all"

180 **dextrae** supply *manui*

181 **usque . . . odio** note the rapid, rolling rhythm of this fully dactylic line, and the rhyme of the words ending in *-o*

illius objective gen. (GL 363.2)

ira the third ablative in the line. Lucilius omits the conjunction this time (asyndeton; GL 473).

185 **haerebat** sing. verb with a compound subject (understandable since the first subject is really a part of the second)

gladium the unusual n. form is the reason the grammarian Nonius quotes this line.

❧ *Human superstition,* Lucilius, *Satires,* fragments 524–29

Here Lucilius ridicules naive belief in gods and spirits. It is tempting to read these lines as the satirist's own commentary, although as with most of the fragments, we do not know who spoke the words in the original poem. The anti-religious sentiment is not unique in Latin literature or thought; for example, Epicurean philosophers, while they believed gods existed, disapproved of religion as a social institution (Lucretius' *On the Nature of Things* expresses this position vehemently). The speaker in Lucilius' fragment is more interested in mocking the inner thoughts of believers.

524 **terriculas Lamias** *et* is omitted between the nouns. *terricula* derives from *terreo*. Lamia is a mythical witch who abducted and devoured children.

Fauni a generalizing pl., like the next: "Faunus, Numa Pompilius, and others like them"

524–25 **Pompilii . . . Numae** the legendary second king of Rome was admired for his piety and his organization of the state religious cults.

525 **instituere** *-ere* is the alternate 3rd person pl. pf. act. indicative ending, especially common in poetry

hic pron., referring to an unknown person in the missing part of the text or perhaps the whole Roman *populus*

omnia ponit "regards as all-important"; another case of asyndeton (cf. note on **181**).

526   **ut** note that an indicative verb follows; "just as." This introduces an analogy that is picked up by *sic* in 527.

infantes in its literal sense: "inarticulate"

credunt introduces an indirect statement

aena here a substantive: "bronze statues." When scanning, note that the initial *a* and *e* are distinct syllables.

527   **isti** Lucilius now generalizes with the pl.: "those [superstitious] folks."

528   **vera putant** another indirect statement; supply *esse*

cor sing. used to denote pl.; this is common in poetry

529   **pergula** supply *est* (and complete the next two phrases in the same way)

pictorum from *pictor*

veri a substantive and a partitive gen. (GL 368)

ꙮ *The Roman rat-race,* Lucilius, *Satires,* fragments 1145–51

In this fragment, one of the longest and best known, Lucilius describes the race for power and influence in Rome. The image of the forum buzzing with competition and dishonest dealings is echoed in some of the later satirists' poems about social competition in the city (e.g., Horace *Satire* 1.6 and 2.6, **Juvenal 3**).

1145   **festo . . . profesto** both modify *die* in 1146

1146   **item pariterque** redundant, perhaps conveying the speaker's agitation

populusque patresque the double -*que* is seen often in poetry (GL 476 N.5d). Juxtaposed with *populus*, *patres* designates senators.

1147   **iactare** with this and the next two infs., supply *videntur* or simply translate as if indicative

omnes modifies *populusque patresque*

decedere supply *de foro*

nusquam may have a temporal sense here ("at no point in time")

1148   **uni . . . eidem . . . studio . . . arti** indirect objects of *se . . . dedere* (from *dedo*)

1149   **verba dare** "cheat"

ut . . . possint the clause defines *uni . . . eidem studio . . . et arti* (GL 557)

caute i.e., in a way that avoids bad consequences; with impunity

1150   **blanditia** abl., either of specification ("compete at flattery") or of means

bonum . . . virum se supply *esse*. The sing. is generalizing, still referring to the plural subject.

1151   **insidias** the direct object of *facere*

ut si "as if"

∾ *A definition of virtue,* Lucilius, *Satires,* fragments 1196–1208

Lucilius defines *virtus* (literally "the character of a true man"), connecting abstract terms to specific aspects of Roman life and customs, such as business and legal dealings and the traditional patron-client relationship. Note the steady pace maintained by the simple presentation of one idea per line, sometimes with repetition in the phrasing. The Christian author Lactantius quotes Lucilius' definition approvingly (*Divine Institutes* 6.5.2). It is possible, however, that the original poem mocked the old-fashioned speaker of these lines (who is as likely to be a pretentious aristocrat as a genuine philosopher).

1196   **virtus . . . est** several lines in the passage will echo this sentence structure, most omitting the *est* (1199, 1201–3)

1197   **quis** alternate form of *quibus* common in poetry (identifiable by the long *i*); an abl. governed by *in* and with the postponed antecedent *rebus*. An unpoetic revision may be helpful: *in illis rebus in quis versamur (et in quis) vivimus.*

potesse an archaic form of *posse*, and the predicate that follows *est*

1197-98 **rebus ... res** the first instance of the word has the sense "business (affairs, dealings)," but the second may be a more general "matters." The whole passage puts the range of connotations of *res* on display, but more subtly than it unpacks *virtus*.

1198   **homini** dat. of interest, as in 1199; in both instances, it is part of the indirect question

quaeque f. sing. of **quisque**

1199   **rectum utile ... honestum** asyndeton; *quid sit* applies to each in turn

1201   **re** here an old form for gen. *rei*, and with the sense "material wealth"

1202   **divitiis ... persolvere** we return to the idea of paying out what is due; *divitiis* is ambiguous, but probably an abl. of means

1203   **re ipsa** "in fact"

1204   **inimicum** used substantively

malorum modifies both nouns (so *bonorum* in 1205)

1205   **contra** adv.

defensorem cf. **Horace 2.5.30** on legal representation, which was indeed a significant part of social and political relations in Republican Rome. Lucilius, however, may be using the term more generally to describe the traditional relationship between an influential man and his dependent clients.

1206   **hos ... his ... his** all refer to the *hominum ... bonorum* of 1205. The first *his* is a dat. of interest, the second a dat. after *amicum*.

magni gen. of value with *facere*; *pretii* is implied, and the phrase means "value highly"

bene velle "wish well for"

1207 **commoda . . . putare** note the alliteration. Read as *putare commoda patriai prima* (*commoda*) *esse*, translating *commoda* as a substantive

      patriai an archaic form of the gen. sing. (GL 29 N.2). Note that the final *a* and *i* scan separately as two long syllables.

1208 **parentum** supply *commoda . . . nostrorum*, to parallel the construction in the previous line; similarly, supply *commoda* with *nostra* later in the line. Duty to parents (*pietas*) is one of the most celebrated Roman virtues, although as this list suggests, even familial demands do not always coincide with the demands of the *patria*.

      iam here in the sense "finally," "only then"

∾ Greed and its manifestations, Horace *Satire* 1.1.41–79

The first poem of Horace's first book of *Satires* is a diatribe on two related vices, discontent and greed. While Horace does not formally introduce and describe the satiric genre in this poem, he makes one point that seems programmatic for the book as a whole: the warning at lines 69–70 that observing the folly of others should lead people to consider their own cases. His overall argument and his style in the poem merit a close reading, since he presents the poem as his debut in satire (although he did not necessarily compose this poem first). Following some conventions of the Hellenistic philosophical diatribe, Horace rolls out caricatures of misguided people, superficially amusing anecdotes with underlying morals, and colorful animal analogies—thus fulfilling his objective of "telling the truth with a laugh" (1.1.24). The selection included here allows us to appreciate the striking physicality of Horace's descriptions of human behavior. The passage does not just present abstract ideas. Horace's fools dig great holes and drink in gulps; they gape with excitement at coins and shudder with fear as they count up potential threats; we see marching slaves and raging rivers, and hear hissing crowds and the protests of the ignorant. Such lively illustrations must have helped the real ancient philosophers who practiced diatribe keep their audiences entertained. Horace's style often mimics oral conversation, with casual transitions from one point or illustration to another ("or how about this . . . ," "it's just like . . ."). But there is remarkable art behind this textual diatribe. The careful and subtle composition produces meaningful word arrangement and sound effects. Horace also shifts between gently musing and creating tension: for example, he stages arguments with his hypothetical greedy man, and even unexpectedly chides him—or is he addressing us, his readers?—for laughing at the fate of Tantalus.

41   **quid iuvat** the acc. *quid* expresses the internal object of the verb ("what help does it provide"; GL 333.2)

    te subject of *deponere*

    argenti . . . et auri partitive gens. with *pondus*

42   **defossa . . . terra** indicates the place where the *pondus* will be stored, but the pple. also denotes an action prior to *deponere* (so: "dig up earth and entrust . . . to it")

43   **quod si** "but if"; Horace is imagining the miser raising an objection

    comminuas understand the stash of money as direct object, though it becomes the subject of *redigatur*

44   **ni id fit** "but if (that reduction) *doesn't* happen"; Horace is speaking again

    quid the object of *habet*; takes a partitive gen.

45   **triverit** pf. subjunctive indicating a concession or assumption ("it may have threshed out"); therefore supply "nevertheless" in the next line

    milia understand this as modifying an unexpressed "measures" or "bushels." The number goes with the partitive gen. *frumenti.*

46   **hoc** causal abl. summing up the previous line: "because of this," "for this reason"

ut si "just as, if . . ."

47   **panis** gen. sing.

venalis acc. pl. (the *-is* ending appears often in the Horace passages). This adj. is used substantively to denote slaves being marched to the market to be sold. Horace passes off the analogy lightly, but the attentive reader may wonder if he is implying that all humans are like powerless slaves as they make their way through life.

inter with *venalis*, and with the sense "as one of"

48   **nihilo** abl. of degree of difference, not comparison (*plus* is followed by *quam*)

48-49   **accipias . . . portarit** note the different tenses (*portarit* is the syncopated form of *portaverit*). The pres. verb refers to a meal taken after the march has ended, the pf. to the march itself.

49   **vel** suggests that the previous illustration should have been sufficient to make the point, but Horace is willing to provide another

referat from *refert*, which takes a dat. of interest here instead of the usual gen. or abl. The verb's subject is the indirect question in 50–51; supply *utrum* after the comma.

49-50   **intra naturae finis viventi** *finis* is acc. pl. The same idea is conveyed in line 75. Most of the major Greco-Roman philosophical schools considered *natura* to be the most legitimate authority on human needs and limits, though they defined its rules in different ways.

51   **ex . . . tollere** "draw from"

52   **parvo** supply *acervo*

nobis . . . haurire relinquas a poetic construction in which *relinquere* has the sense "allow" (+ inf. and dat.)

54   **ut . . . si** cf. line 46

tibi dat. of possession with *sit*

sit opus usually takes an abl. denoting the thing needed, but here looks to *non amplius* first; the abls. (of comparison) follow

liquidi partitive gen. with *urna* and *cyatho*

55   **mallem** supply an unexpressed protasis: "if I had a choice" (B 280.4)

56   **eo** like *hoc* in 46

56-57   **fit . . . ut** introduces a substantive clause; *plenior* belongs inside this clause.

57   **si quos** note that *ali-* is dropped from the pronoun after *si*. The subjunctive in the clause implies that Horace is referring to a general type, not specific individuals.

58   **avulsos** refers to the people described in the *si* clause

   Aufidus a river in Apulia, Horace's native region (see map); in springtime it no doubt swelled and flowed rapidly

59   **qui . . . is** the indicative verbs in both clauses emphasize that such a person exists

60   **tantuli . . . quanto** the case of *tantuli* is governed by *eget*, that of *quanto* by *est opus*. *tantuli* may be wordplay, foreshadowing the Tantalus exemplum in lines 68–69; both passages describe someone being thwarted by rushing water.

61   **bona pars** "the majority"; a sing. collective subject

   decepta takes an abl. of means (cf. *limo turbatum*, 59–60)

62   **nil satis est** *satis* is a key word in Horace's *Satires*: not only is it appropriate to discussions of greed and limits such as this one, but it is etymologically connected to "satire." Horace ends this poem declaring *iam satis est* about his own diatribe (line 120); this may be an etymological joke suggesting that even the "stuffed" genre needs to operate within limits.

   tanti gen. of value (take with *sis*) and correlative with *quantum*. Compare the thought with Lucilius 1194–95: *aurum atque ambitio specimen virtuti' virique est:/ quantum habeas, tantum ipse sies tantique habearis.*

   sis generalizing 2nd person. With the subjunctive, the speaker suggests that this is popular opinion rather than proven fact (but compelling enough to him).

63   **illi** dat. sing., although *facio* in this expression usually takes an abl. Notice that the man in Horace's example has shifted from a "you" to a "he"; the satirist is now trying to make his reader feel part of an "in" group.

iubeas miserum esse can be translated two ways: either "tell him to go ahead and be wretched," or—as a play on the idiom *iubere valere*—bid him fare-ill"

libenter modifies *facit* in 64

64   **ut** "just as"

Athenis locative. An anecdote set in Athens is fitting in a poem that imitates the originally Greek diatribe tradition—and in a story that employs a theatrical metaphor (*sibilat . . . plaudo*, 66), since Athens was the birthplace of Greek drama.

66   **sic** points to the quote. The *s* sounds in this and the previous line conjure the hissing *populus*.

me *sibilat* usually takes a dat., like *plaudo*

67   **simul ac** almost implies that public attacks regularly drive the miser home to his *arca* for consolation

68   **Tantalus** Horace shifts to a mythological exemplum. The king Tantalus abused his close relationship to the gods, either by stealing their nectar and ambrosia or (in other accounts) by feeding them his own child to test them. All accounts agree on his punishment in the underworld: he was placed in a pool with water and food constantly receding just out of his reach. The receding surface of the (still) pool is appropriately described as *flumina*.

fugientia the sense is completed by *a labris*

captat the frequentative form implies eternal failure

69   **quid rides** Horace imagines his interlocutor, or perhaps his reader, mocking the exemplum. *quid* is the direct object, but may also be rendered as "why?"

mutato nomine abl. absolute

de te the spondee at the end of the line makes Horace's warning sound even more severe

70   **fabula** i.e., the Tantalus story

congestis . . . saccis probably a dat. to be taken after *indormis*, but may also be translated as if it were an abl. absolute

undique modifies the pple.

71   **inhians** reflects excitement or anxiety

et "and yet," "and at the same time." Horace is targeting irrationality as much as immorality.

tamquam take with *sacris*, which Horace uses substantively ("sacred objects")

72   **cogeris** with middle sense: "force yourself" (+ inf.)

73   **quo** literally "to what end," "for what purpose"

74   **panis** nom. sing.

ematur the subjunctive is either potential or jussive

75   **quis** *quibus* (see note on **Lucilius 1197**). A prosaic rendering of 75–76 would be *adde ea quibus negatis* (an abl. absolute with conditional sense) *sibi* (referring to *natura*) *humana natura doleat.*

76-77 **an vigilare . . . formidare** supply *te*. The two infs. will be summed up in the sing. *hoc* in 78.

noctesque diesque acc. of extent of time

77   **incendia** mentioned as a common source of fear at **Juvenal 3.197**

78   **ne . . . fugientes** fearing clause, elaborating on *formidare . . . servos*

iuvat here "pleases" or "is your preference"

78-79 **horum . . . bonorum** the separation of the words may seem odd, but the position of *horum* makes clear that it refers to lines 76–78, while the delay of *bonorum* (a substantive) makes for a striking and sarcastic conclusion to the thought

79   **optarim** syncopated form of *optaverim*. The pf. subjunctive implies a fut. condition (supply "should I be given the choice"); contrast with the impf. subjunctive in 55.

pauperrimus takes a gen. of fullness (GL 374)

∾ *Horace defends his satire,* Horace *Satire* 1.4.103–43

In the first three poems of *Satires* book 1, Horace introduces himself to the reader indirectly through his brand of moral criticism; in the fourth, he gives a more explicit self-introduction and self-defense. He claims that his satire is inspired by his own father's homespun moralizing, a routine of his childhood, and is geared mainly toward his own self-improvement. There is an implicit parallel between the literary model of Lucilius (whom Horace evaluates in the opening of the poem) and Horace's more literal satiric forefather: both men inspired Horace, but both practiced an unedited and outspoken kind of moral criticism, while he himself aims for polish and discretion. As usual in Horace, there is more art to this argument than is immediately apparent. The vivid portrait of Horace's parent seems to be modeled on the stern, frugal fathers of Roman comedy (Demea in Terence's *Brothers* being the most obvious example), and this resemblance hints at the diverse literary recipe of Horace's satire. It should also remind us that even Horace's self-portrait in the *Satires* is a poetic construction, however much continuity it may show from poem to poem. Finally, despite the smugness of Horace's self-defense here, elsewhere he elaborates on the "minor vices" that he has retained despite his father's efforts. In the passages from **Satire 2.7,** the slave Davus claims that the poet is not only flawed but hypocritical. Horace's checkered self-portrait serves to warn readers that the satirist figure should not be mistaken for a moral paragon.

103-4   **liberius ... iocosius** not true comparatives, but in the sense "a bit too . . . ." Take *dixero* and *forte* with each.

104   **iuris** partitive gen. with *hoc*

105   **hoc** either acc., functioning as a second object of *insuevit*, or abl., expressing means and referring to the practice described in the lines to come

106   **quaeque** acc. pl. n. of *quisque*, taking a partitive gen. (*vitiorum*); it serves as the direct object of both *fugerem* and *notando*

Fig. 4. Terracotta figurines of two comic actors playing a male slave and a *paterfamilias* (Etruria, Republican period).

107   **cum . . . hortaretur** the impf. subjunctive suggests a frequent occurrence. *hortaretur* looks to *uti* (= *ut*).

108   **parasset** syncopated form of *paravisset*

109-11 **nonne . . . velit** supply *aiebat* from line 115 with this and all the quotations of Horace's father

109   **vides . . . ut male vivat** indirect question; *ut* = "how." *Albi* is the contracted form of gen. *Albii*, suited to the metrical scheme here.

110 **magnum documentum** supply *hoc est*; a negative purpose clause follows

 rem "material property"

111 **amore** probably referring to an attachment of some duration, as we see between youths and prostitutes in many Roman comedies. Earlier in the book, *Satire* 1.2, Horace had criticized two "extreme" and unwise choices of female love object: the cheapest prostitutes and married women. The current passage creates the impression that Horace derived his topic from his father's lectures.

112 **Scetani dissimilis sis** scan to see how rough the command sounds, with stress accent and metrical accent jerkily conflicting and the line ending in a monosyllable. Horace may be trying to convey the bluntness and abruptness of his father's lectures.

113 **concessa . . . venere** abl. after *uti* (from *utor*). The sense of *concessa* is "legitimate, lawful"—i.e., unlike sex with married women. Adulterous Roman wives and their partners could be lawfully subjected to harsh private vengeance, as *Satire* 1.2 illustrates.

114 **deprensi** gen. modifying *Treboni*. The pple. may be translated with temporal sense; it explains how Trebonius acquired his *fama*.

115 **vitatu quidque petitu** in prosaic wording, *quid vitatu quidque* (= *quid + -que*) *petitu*. The acc. prons. express respect ("as to what"). The supines are abls. of specification, qualifying *melius* in 116.

116 **causas** i.e., philosophically based theories and arguments. In contrast, Horace's father models a homespun and practical wisdom.

117 **ab antiquis** follows (*morem*) *traditum*; *antiquis* is a substantive (m.) here

117-18 **servare . . . tueri** take with *possum* in 119

119 **incolumem** like *tuam*, applies to both fem. sing. acc. nouns in 118. The adj. is used proleptically or predicatively after *tueri* (GL 325).

120   **tuum** in sense, goes with both *membra* and *animum*

      cortice evidently a large piece of cork, the Roman version of a kickboard or water-wings

121   **puerum** with the sense "as a boy," "in my boyhood"

      sive this and the *sive* in 124 introduce independent, but parallel, conditions

      iubebat takes an *ut* clause instead of the usual acc. and inf.

122   **auctorem** "a (good) example"; the antecedent of *quo*

123   **unum . . . obiciebat** the apodosis of the condition

      iudicibus selectis evokes the official procedure of jury selection in Roman courts

124   **sive vetabat** understand "then he would say" before the quote (the apodosis)

124-26 **an . . . hic atque ille** take care in translating the separate clauses. *an* governs *addubites*, a potential subjunctive. This in turn sets up an indirect alternative question ("whether or not this is . . ."). A *cum* clause follows; *malo rumore* modifies *flagret*. Horace's father hopes his son will answer "no" to the framing direct question (*addubites . . .* ?)

127   **exanimat** used figuratively, but a clever word choice for people watching a funeral

      sibi parcere "take care of themselves"

129   **ex hoc** not temporal, but causal, referring to long practice

      sanus ab illis supply *vitiis*, an abl. of separation in an unparalleled but plausible construction with *sanus*

130   **quis** *quibus* (see note on **Lucilius 1197**); the object of *ignoscas* in 131

131   **istinc** i.e., *ex istis mediocribus vitiis*

132   **liber amicus** the sing. can still refer to repeat occurrences

133   **proprium** "my own," developed from experience

133-34 **cum lectulus aut . . . porticus excepit** i.e., while Horace is dining or strolling

134   **desum mihi** "neglect myself," "fail myself"

134-36   **hoc . . . hoc . . . sic . . . hoc** these represent Horace's observations on different occasions

135   **dulcis** nom. sing.

136   **hoc . . . non belle** supply *facit* or *dicit*

        numquid note that the *num* introduces a question; the *quid* stands for *aliquid* (cf. *quid* with partitive gen. in 138)

137   **inprudens** this word derives from *provideo*, "look ahead" or "foresee"; thus *inprudentia* can be a preventable failure of judgment, not just pure ignorance

138   **ubi quid datur oti** sc. *mihi. ubi* has temporal sense here.

139   **illudo chartis** *chartis* is dat. following the compound verb; the phrase can be translated "playfully throw on paper" or "waste paper." Horace repeatedly, and disingenuously, characterizes satire as a sub-literary form.

139-40   **hoc est . . . unum** another self-deprecating characterization of the practice of satire. It leads abruptly to a mock threat against the genre's critics and an assertion that its practitioners are indeed *poetae*.

141-42   **auxilio . . . mihi** double dat. (GL 356). It belongs inside the rel. clause, which expresses purpose.

142   **multo plures sumus** Persius and Juvenal also imply that Rome was veritably choked with poets

142-43   **veluti . . . Iudaei** a great many Jews lived in Rome in Horace's time, but it does not seem that they actively proselytized; Horace is promoting a stereotype

∾ *How to hunt legacies,* Horace *Satire* 2.5.23–50

Uniquely among Horace's *Satires*, 2.5 has a mythological setting. It parodies book 11 of Homer's *Odyssey*, the episode in which the wandering hero Odysseus consults the ghost of the seer Tiresias to learn how he can reclaim his home. In Horace's poem the hero (Ulysses in Latin) is placed in a thoroughly sordid, modern, and Roman context.

In this setting he is specifically concerned with recovering his lost wealth, and is advised by the prophet to court rich childless people looking for heirs—that is, to join the ranks of unscrupulous, manipulative legacy-hunters (*captatores*). Childless rich people who attract flatterers do appear here and there in historical accounts of late Republican and Imperial Rome; the emperor Augustus may have hoped to discourage *captatores* when he passed laws encouraging members of the nobility to have children, although not all nobles were rich. But the *captator* becomes a satiric type in his own right in Persius, Juvenal, and Petronius. The cynicism with which Horace endows the traditionally pious prophet is a shocking and amusing touch: Tiresias sounds like an unsavory motivational speaker as he urges Ulysses to work tirelessly at his goal. He encourages the hero to see his victims not as humans but as prey, although he guesses, perhaps correctly, that they will respond only too readily to the fawning *captator* (line 44). Ulysses' role here is somehow less surprising, since he is portrayed throughout Greek and Roman literature as practical and ruthless, focused on achieving his own and his associates' ends by any means. The entire passage excerpted here comes from Tiresias' long speech.

23   **captes** the verb from which *captator* is formed; the implied object is "legacies," and this may be added to the translation

24   **vafer unus et alter** "one or two clever (rich) men"

25   **praeroso . . . hamo** Tiresias describes the *vafer* as a fish stealing bait and escaping

27   **foro** abl. of place where

       res here a legal case (*vocet in ius* in 29 means "takes to court")

28   **vivet** equivalent to *erit*; it belongs inside the clause that starts with *uter*

       uter "whichever (party in the case)," the referent of *illius* in 29

       ultro i.e., "without provocation," "brashly"; belongs inside the rel. clause in 29

29   **esto** the fut. imperative of *sum*; this is regular in legal formulas, and so gives this command a mock-legal flavor (GL 268.2)

30 **defensor** one who could shrewdly present the man's case, as Ulysses is instructed to style himself in line 34

fama . . . causaque scanning will reveal the length of the endings; these are abls. of specification modifying *priorem* (which has the sense of *meliorem*)

32 **puta** Tiresias directs Ulysses to imagine the conversation; the command has the sense "suppose" or "for instance"

Publi vocative

molles "sensitive" or more likely "malleable"

34 **ius anceps** "ambiguous (points of) law"

35 **mihi** dat. of disadvantage

36 **contemptum** may be translated verbally before *pauperet* ("slight you and . . .")

cassa nuce i.e., an empty nut, proverbial for a small amount. The abl. denotes separation after *paupero*, an archaic word that fits this (superficially) mythological scene.

38 **pelliculam curare** "coddle himself"; the diminutive oozes concern

39-41 **seu rubra Canicula . . . Alpis** over-the-top poetic ways of describing summer and winter. With the reference to the Dog Star "splitting speechless statues" (with its accompanying heat), Horace may be referring to wooden statues placed outdoors, or parodying a lost literary passage (see note on 41).

40 **omaso** either a metaphor for heavy poetry, or a literal reference to this poet's diet

41 **Furius** according to ancient commentary on this text, this is Furius Bibaculus, a poet of the mid-second century BCE whose work has been lost. Horace mocks that poet in a similar way at *Satire* 1.10.36–37. Here, Horace imagines the poet who describes a winter landscape (inelegantly, as implied by *conspuet*) as bringing on winter himself.

42 **prope** modifies *stantem*

43   **ut . . . ut . . . ut** "how," in parallel indirect questions; supply *sit*
      with each

44   **adnabunt . . . crescent** the fishing metaphor returns. A tun-
      ny-fish (tuna) could be quite large, like the desired "catch" of
      the *captator*. Stocked fish ponds make for an easy harvest.

45   **male** modifies *validus*, with the sense "insufficiently," "not
      quite." Tiresias is explaining how to exploit a delicate situation.

46   **sublatus aletur** a father acknowledged a newborn as his own
      by picking it up (the official gesture known as *tollere*) and so
      agreeing to raise it (*alere*)

47   **caelibis** a substantive; objective gen. after *obsequium*

47-48 **leniter in spem adrepe** the hope is described in 48–50 (a sub-
      stantive clause). The *captator* should be prepared to achieve
      his goal in two steps. A will would need to name a *secundus
      heres* in case the principal heir died before inheriting; the sec-
      ond heir would take the "empty place" (*vacuum*, 50).

48   **officiosus** may be translated adverbially, or as a separate com-
      mand: "(be) attentive (and)"

49   **casus** nom. sing., going with *quis*

      Orco technically a personal name, but here equated with a
      place (the underworld) and used in the dat. to denote place to
      which (GL 358)

∾ *The satirist in the hot seat,* Horace *Satire* 2.7.21–71

The second book of *Satires* contains many poems that feature the
poet himself in passive or disadvantaged positions, demonstrating
that satire can work in many forms other than head-on attack and
mockery. Horace the character is entirely absent in **2.5**, and elsewhere where he is present, he receives advice or stories from others.
In 2.3 and 2.7 he is the target of long moral diatribes, and in the latter,
the satirist's slave Davus speaks. The setting is the Saturnalia holiday
(when the master-slave hierarchy was temporarily overturned), and

Davus takes advantage of the atmosphere to lecture his master on morality—and specifically, on the Stoic idea of sin as metaphorical slavery. As Horace's father in **1.4** is modeled on a comic type, Davus is reminiscent of some outspoken slaves in Plautus and Terence. Horace also makes himself into a comic figure: Davus charges him with inconsistency, hypocrisy, adultery, and a bad temper. Horace's critical portrayal of himself here makes an ironic epilogue to the claims at **1.4.103–43,** and a fitting climax to a book of poems that seems to dramatize Horace's abrogation of the satirist's role. It makes sense for Horace to portray his own house slave—someone trained virtually to read his master's mind—as an adept satirist himself. The reader may compare Davus' positions and style of delivery to Horace's in the selection from **1.1**.

21-22 **non dices . . . furcifer** Horace speaks here, after Davus has rattled off a number of general moral statements. As the poet himself does at **1.1.69–70**, the slave is about to reveal that the sermon actually applies personally to his interlocutor.

21 **quorsum** begins the indirect question. Horace may mean "to what conclusion?" but Davus takes him to mean "at whom?"

22 **quo pacto** "in what way"

23 **et idem** "yet you, the same man, also . . ."

24 **illa** refers to *fortunam et mores antiquae plebis*

25 **rectius esse** indirect statement. It may be translated twice, after *sentis* and *clamare*.

26-27 **haeres . . . plantam** a proverbial and comic image (cf. Plautus *Bacchides* 384)

27 **nequiquam** modifies *cupiens*

28 **Romae rus optas** exactly as Horace pictures himself praying in the previous poem, where he praises his Sabine villa as a retreat from stressful city life: *o rus, quando ego ad te aspiciam?* (*Satire* 2.6.60)

   rusticus functions parallel to *Romae*: "when you are in the country"

29   **levis** nom. sing.; postponed to be the final dig of the sentence

30   **securum** a transferred epithet; the person who eats *holus* en-
        joys the "quiet" life

30-31   **velut usquam vinctus eas** this hint gives way to a more explic-
        it description. Davus insinuates that Horace plays the parasite
        to his patron Maecenas (on parasites, see the note on **Juvenal
        1.139**).

32   **iusserit** a jussive subjunctive that functions like the protasis
        of a condition (B 305.2). The apodosis is an understood "you
        say" (before the quote at 34–35).

33   **serum** modifying Horace, a "last-minute" addition to the
        guest list, but indicting Maecenas' etiquette as well

34   **nemon** *nemo* + *-ne*

        oleum needed for the torches that Horace will use on his trek
        to Maecenas' house, having only been invited *sub lumina pri-
        ma* ("at first lamp-lighting time")

        ocius "good and quick" (cf. line 117)

35   **audit** "is listening"

        blateras this is the only instance of this verb (an apparent
        onomatopoeia) in extant Latin literature

36   **Mulvius** one of the *scurrae*; Davus puts words in his mouth,
        cleverly making yet another party "do satire"

        non referenda "unmentionable," the direct object of *precati*.
        tibi is a dat. of disadvantage.

37   **dixerit** may be translated as an ordinary fut. It suggests a
        missing protasis: "if you ask him . . ."

37-38   **me . . . duci . . . levem** an indirect statement after *fateor*; Mul-
        vius next switches to direct discourse

38   **nasum** the object of *supinor*, which has a middle sense

        nidore specifically, the aroma of cooking

39   **si quid . . . popino** Davus allows one more label for himself

40   **cum** concessive

quod ego supply *sum*

nequior compar. of *nequam* (indecl.)

ultro indicating that Horace is not only flawed himself (as expressed in the *cum* clause), but also attacks other people; cf. **2.5.28**

41 **insectere** 2nd sing. pres. subjunctive; like *obvolvas*, a potential subjunctive that expresses Davus' incredulity

velut melior referring to Horace; *sis* may be supplied for sense

verbis . . . decoris the description is wonderfully scathing. Davus has become a satirist in the spirit of Lucilius, who according to Horace stripped the false facades off his targets (*Satire* 2.1.64–65).

42 **quid** "what to think?" Davus is now speaking as himself again.

42-43 **stultior . . . deprenderis** "you are discovered (to be) more foolish"

43 **quingentis . . . drachmis** abl. of price with *empto*. The sum, equivalent to about 2,000 sesterces, was not a high price for a slave. Davus names his price in the Greek unit of currency as if he were a character in one of the Greek-style comedies of Plautus or Terence.

aufer "stop," "don't" (+ inf.)

44 **stomachum** a mundane term for "temper"; cf. Horace *Ode* 1.6.6

teneto 2nd person sing. fut. imperative

45 **Crispini . . . ianitor** Crispinus was apparently a tedious Stoic lecturer and an equally tedious poet; Horace refers mockingly to his run-on style at *Satire* 1.1.120–21, 1.3.138–39, and 1.4.13–16. Davus' reference to the source of his own enlightenment is a humorous surprise, although there is some logic to the idea of a poet's slave learning from a philosopher's doorman. The *ianitor* and Davus both appear capable of taking their masters' places.

edo the word conveys solemnity and gravity

46   **te coniunx . . . capit** Davus begins to analyze his master's behavior. He implies that the warnings of Horace's father at **1.4.113–14** did not entirely succeed.

   capit cf. Propertius 1.1.1 on his attraction to his mistress: *Cynthia . . . suis . . . me cepit ocellis*

   meretricula supply *capit*. This is the other type of unwise affair criticized by Horace's father at **1.4.111–12**. Horace himself mocks attachments to prostitutes in *Satire* 1.2. Davus argues that there are greater and lesser offenses when it comes to erotic passion.

47   **nostrum** gen. pl., governed by *uter*

   dignius compar. adv.

   acris nom. sing.

47–48   **acris . . . me natura intendit** obliquely describes an erection, but the obliqueness is replaced by crude slang in 49–50 (*cauda = penis*). Davus clearly takes pride in conducting his legitimate sexual business *sub clara . . . lucerna* (48), and in describing it with equal frankness. *nuda* and *lasciva* (48–49) each add further detail and are best translated separately.

49–50   **quaecumque excepit . . . verbera . . . aut agitavit equum** "whatever woman happens to have taken the poundings . . . or shaken (me in the role of) the horse . . ."

49   **turgentis** modifies *caudae*

50   **clunibus** abl. of means

51   **dimittit** supply *me*. This confirms that Davus has been with a prostitute, and one who is not likely to bring in rich or attractive clients (as implied in the subsequent clause of fearing).

52   **formae melioris** a gen. of description or quality, modifying an unexpressed (*ali*)*quis* and parallel in function to *ditior*

   meiat vulgar for "ejaculate." *eodem* denotes place.

53   **cum** the conj., introducing *prodis* in the next line

   proiectis insignibus abl. absolute; *insignibus* refers to the next two abls. The usual emblem of equestrian status is a plain gold ring. It is uncertain whether Horace held equestrian status by this time; if not, Davus' *tu* is more generalizing.

54   **Romano habitu** i.e., a white toga

      ex iudice "instead of a juror" (*iudex* here denotes a trustworthy citizen)

      Dama a common slave name seen in legal and literary sources; modified by *turpis* in 55

56   **quod simulas** Davus means that Horace goes out for his assignations disguised as a slave, and he finds this ironically appropriate (cf. line 113). The Stoics used slavery as a metaphor for the power vices hold over those who practice them. With very different aims, the Roman love elegists depicted their passion as *servitium* to their mistresses and to love itself.

57   **ossa** acc. of the part affected: "in your bones"

58   **quid refert** introduces an indirect question; supply *utrum* to parallel *an* in 59

58-59 **uri . . . necari . . . auctoratus eas** i.e., whether you literally sell yourself into slavery as a gladiator

59-61 **an . . . tangas caput** comic dramatic genres, particularly the popular mime (not a silent performance but a lively play), often depicted unfaithful wives and their lovers sneaking about; cf. the final scene of Plautus' *Braggart Soldier*, where slaves chase the would-be adulterer away, and the tales in book 9 of Apuleius' *Metamorphoses*. Roman law allowed husbands to exact violent revenge on men whom they caught *in flagrante delicto* with their wives (and on their wives; cf. *in ambo*, 62). Davus' vivid account evokes the comic literary scenario more than the real-life legal one, although it leads to a stern warning.

59   **turpi** "disreputable" because it is a conventional hiding-place for adulterers

60   **quo** "the place into which (she thrust you)," i.e., the *arca*

      demisit note that this verb implies debasement or confinement, whereas Davus' *dimittit* in line 51 suggests liberation

       conscia modifying an unexpressed *ancilla*, a familiar character from comedy and mime and the accomplice in many a household plot

61   **estne** the language of Roman comedy (Davus' idiom) uses *ne* where classical Latin would use *nonne. est* is used in a possessive construction with *marito* (dat.).

62   **matronae peccantis** possessive gen.; take with *marito*

       in here "over," "with respect to"

63   **corruptorem** the adulterer. Davus underscores his base behavior by arguing for the wife's lesser guilt.

64   **habitu mutatve loco** understand as (*se*) *mutat habitu locove*; then *peccatve* (with the *-ve* meaning "or" or "nor") parallels *mutat*

       superne may mean "by lying on top," implying a perversion of the same degree as the slave disguise. The text here is uncertain, however; some editors read *peccatque* and understand the phrase to mean "and (she *does*) sin in a higher (i.e., less morally offensive) way."

65   **cum** concessive, drawing a contrast between the two parties to the crime

       mulier presumably explains *formidet*: "because she is a woman"

66   **furcam** "the fork" means "the stocks," a slave's punishment

       domino appropriately ambiguous: the "master of the house" (the husband) is now the slavish adulterer's "master"

67   **rem** "your property," also at risk if the husband discovers the adultery

68   **credo** sarcastic: "I suppose"

69   **quaeres quando** "you will go looking for an opportunity to"

71   **prava** can be translated adverbially; sums up the entire action described

∾ *The satirist in the hot seat* (continued), Horace *Satire* 2.7.111–18

The poem ends abruptly when Horace flares up in anger, and reminds Davus of his slave status. The Saturnalian atmosphere is dissolved, but Horace does not escape unscathed or without demonstrating some of the flaws Davus has identified in him. Moreover, in the next and last poem in the book, he will (albeit cheerfully) play the part of a social outsider and a listener to satiric narrative instead of an author. By the end of book 2, then, Horace has fleshed out the image of the satirst as a flawed and vulnerable figure and so created an interesting model for future practitioners of the genre.

111   **quod** "the fact that"

112-13   **non horam . . . et erro** contentment with oneself is a central goal in Stoic ethics (see especially Seneca's dialogue *De tranquillitate*). *horam* (acc. of extent of time) may be a pun on Horace's name. Note the anaphora with *non* (cf. *iam . . . iam* in 114); Davus is still hammering eloquently away at his argument as his time runs out. With *fugitivus et erro*, the slavery metaphor continues.

113   **ponere** "dispose of," "use"

114   **fallere curam** "while away your care," governed by *quaerens* and taking abls. of means

115   **comes atra** i.e., death; cf. *Satire* 2.1.58: *Mors atris circumvolat alis*

       fugacem we can supply *te*, but may also note that the more abstract formulation works, as in Horace *Odes* 3.2.14, *mors et fugacem persequitur virum*. Note the urgent dactylic rhythm of the line.

116   **unde . . . lapidem . . . unde sagittas** Horace breaks in, in colloquial style; supply *parem* or a similar verb

       quorsum est opus Davus interrupting smugly, with an amusing echo of Horace's complaint at line 21

117   **aut insanit . . . aut versus facit** this cryptic observation (a private joke between master and slave?) suggests that to Davus, the two conditions are not dissimilar; satire-writing is violent in its own way

118   **opera . . . nona** in apposition to the subject. The significance of the number is not clear. Horace's final threat recalls the punishment that the slaves in Roman comedy fear most.

❧ *A self-sufficient satirist,* Persius *Satire* 1.1–12

Persius introduces himself as a cheeky mocker of Roman pretension, and as an author who is aiming not for popularity but for his own amusement. Horace also claims not to care for a large audience (though we know that both poets recited their work to appreciative friends), and also like Horace, Persius sometimes characterizes satire as casual or sub-literary. In each case, the author's poetic art belies such claims. After this opening passage, Persius goes on to mock men who compose and critique poetry, preening themselves as they regurgitate the trendy poetic principles of the day. The subject is fitting for a programmatic satire, in which the poet is asserting—if often subtly—his own special literary credentials.

1   **o curas hominum** acc. of exclamation. The ancient commentary on Persius tells us that the poet "took this verse from the first book of Lucilius." Editors of Lucilius accordingly include this passage in collections of the fragments, although they note that it is not certain whether "took" (*transtulit*) means "quoted" or "adapted," or even whether the commentary refers to a single phrase or multiple lines. It would be an interesting beginning for Persius to start with a quotation from satire's founding father.

2   **quis leget haec** an interlocutor interrupts the poet's rhetorical questions

       min *mihi* + *-ne*

3   **duo** used indefinitely to designate a small number

4-5   **ne . . . praetulerint** a response to *turpe et miserabile*; imagine Persius preceding this with "should I be afraid/bothered lest . . ."

4   **Polydamas et Troiades** Persius adapts the phrase from Homer's *Iliad* 22.99–107, where the panicking Hector regrets defying the advice of the Trojan Polydamas and making his people vulnerable to a Greek assault. The epic allusion may be a gesture to the members of the Roman aristocracy (supposedly descended from Trojans) who sometimes provided funds and publicity to chosen poets. The image of male nobles as "Trojan ladies" adds to the joke.

    Labeonem a translator of Homer's epics, according to the ancient commentary

5   **nugae** Persius is dismissing his critics' judgment, but many students will recall the use of this word as a mock-modest term for poetry in Catullus (1.4)

5-7   **non . . . accedas . . . castiges . . . quaesiveris** equivalent to negative commands. *accedas* has the sense "agree with." The *-ve* attached to *examen* in 6 actually connects the first two verbs.

6   **elevet** "make light of," "deem worthless"; introducing the metaphor of the scale. It takes the object *quid* (= *aliquid*) in 5.

7   **nec te quaesiveris extra** ambiguous; *te* can taken with *extra*, but it may or may not serve as the direct object as well. Thus the two possible meanings are "nor seek yourself outside (yourself)" and "nor seek (anything) outside yourself." Either way the command stresses self-sufficiency.

8   **nam Romae quis non** sc. *est*? the question is interrupted (aposiopesis; GL 691) and only completed at line 121, after Persius has satirized the behavior and ideas of poetry audiences in Rome

    si . . . sed fas "if only it were right, but (really) it *is* right . . ."

9   **nostrum istud vivere triste** the inf. is a substantive modified by *triste*: "that strict (way of) living of ours"

10   **aspexi** takes three objects: first an acc. noun, then an inf., and last an indirect question

      nucibus . . . relictis abl. absolute. Roman sources refer to children's toys as "nuts." The term may denote small stones or pieces of bone used as marbles.

11   **cum sapimus patruos** difficult to translate. *sapere* takes an acc. object and means "taste like" or "have the characteristics of." Many translate "when we have started smacking of (serious old) uncles."

11-12   **tunc . . . faciam** Persius interrupts himself again, and then again with the parenthesis. Supply "but" or "yet" after the comma. *faciam* is deliberative subjunctive.

12   **petulanti splene** abl. of description or quality

      cachinno this verb is not seen in other authors, and so may be a coinage of Persius'; some editors prefer to see it as a dat. of the noun *cachinnus*, following *ignoscite* (supply "my")

∾ *A self-sufficient satirist* (continued), Persius *Satire* 1.107–34

After mocking the literary endeavors and attitudes of his contemporaries in a long and often obscure passage, Persius returns to his own case to end his programmatic poem. He places himself in the tradition of Horace, Lucilius, and Greek Old Comedy (i.e., the fiercely irreverent and linguistically sophisticated plays of Aristophanes and others), and describes his ideal reader.

107-10   **sed quid . . . littera** the speaker is Persius' critical interlocutor. Sc. *est* with *opus*.

107   **vero** a substantive here

108   **auriculas** the diminutive makes the scraping sound all the more painful

      vide sis ne a formula for a negative command ("make sure that . . . not"). The form *sis* (*si vis*, "if you please") is common in the dialogues of Roman comedy.

maiorum in the sense of social betters rather than elders

109 **limina frigescant** a striking image of exclusion that echoes Horace *Satire* 2.1.61–62: *metuo . . . maiorum ne quis amicus / frigore te feriat.* The "thresholds of the great" were the gathering places for clients of lesser status seeking legal and financial aid, and some clients never saw more than their patrons' front doors; cf. Juvenal 1.95–134.

hic the adv., referring to Persius' satire

109-10 **canina littera** simply the letter *r*, the sound a snarling guard dog makes. In a fragment from his first book, Lucilius refers to the *littera inritata canes quam . . . dicit* (3–4), presumably in a discussion of satire similar to this one.

110 **per me** "as far as I'm concerned," reinforced by *equidem*

sint a sarcastic command

alba in symbolic sense: "spotless," "peachy"

111 **nil moror** "I don't trouble myself," "I don't care"

euge a transliteration of the Greek word for "well done"; cf. our use of "bravo." Horace depicts pretentious amateur poets lavishing unwarranted praise on one another at *Art of Poetry* 419–33.

mire eritis res the fut. implies "from here on." *res* is vague, but Persius may be making a joke with the word in its sense "subjects for poetry."

112 **hoc iuvat** the sense is "happy now?"

inquis Persius is still addressing his interlocutor

veto . . . faxit oletum a metaphor for this "emperor's new clothes" scenario. *veto . . . faxit* is legal language (*faxit* is an alternate pf. subjunctive). The satirist is being warned away from "sacred spaces" marked by totems such as paintings of snakes (cf. 113). *oletum* derives from the verb *oleo* ("make a stink").

113 **pueri** a generalizing pl., including the satirist, who is like an impish child

114 **discedo** Persius feigns capitulation—briefly. A new line of defense is coming.

115 **te Lupe, te Muci** the names are in vocative form; this is a brief
direct address (apostrophe) to Lucilius' long-dead targets
Lentulus Lupus and Mucius Scaevola (see Introduction), who
are then replaced by *illis*

genuinum fregit in illis the consequence of zealous biting
(adjusting the sense of *secuit*)

116 **vafer** this term refers to wit and skill as much as to naughti-
ness, although it is more negative at line 130

ridenti . . . amico a dat. of reference; the friend could be Horace's target, his audience, or both

118 **callidus** takes the inf.: "clever at hanging"

excusso "shaken out," metaphorical for "discriminating" (we
might use a different image such as "upturned"). This evokes
Horace's description of Lucilius as *emunctae naris* (*Satire*
1.4.8). The abl. is governed by *suspendere*; the expression
seems to denote mockery.

119 **me muttire nefas** supply *est*

nec "not even"

120 **hic** the adv.; refers to Persius' satire

libelle poets who work in the less grand genres (love poetry,
epigram, satire) often describe their books with the diminutive;
the word underscores the image of Persius' satire as "a trifle"

121 **auriculas . . . habet** finally, the end of the question begun at
line 8. Note the use of the diminutive *auriculas* again (cf. 108).
The image evokes the mythical king Midas, who sprouted ass'
ears as punishment for his flawed artistic judgment. The ancient biography of Persius tells us that the line originally read
auriculas asini Mida rex habet, but was changed by the poet's
editors after his death because *rex* seemed to allude danger-
ously to the emperor Nero (*Life of Persius* lines 56–59). If the
story is true, this would represent a rare *ad hominem* attack in
Persius' work. Nero was indeed famous for his literary preten-
sions; Tacitus tells us that he sought help with his own compositions from lesser-known poets (*Annals* 14.16).

opertum used substantively

122   **hoc ridere meum** a phrase like *nostrum istud vivere triste* in line 9. "This laughter" does not convey the sense of the inf. as well as "this ability/tendency to laugh."

     tam nil hard to translate; "such a trifle" is one option

122-23   **nulla . . . Iliade** abl. of price. Grand epic is again the foil for Persius' refined poetry (cf. lines 4–5).

123-25   **audaci . . . audis** Persius now addresses his ideal reader, characterizing him by the other literature he enjoys and painting him as one who has been refined (mentally and almost physically) by his discriminating choices. There may be intentional wordplay in *audaci* and *audis*, linking the "bold" comic playwrights with the adventurous fan of Persius.

123   **audaci . . . Cratino** one of the acknowledged "big three" Old Comic playwrights from classical Athens; the other two follow in Persius' list. Persius means "you who like Cratinus, Eupolis, and Aristophanes," but creates a striking variation by putting each poet in a different grammatical construction. Horace links satire to Greek Old Comedy at *Satire* 1.4.1–7, claiming that Lucilius followed Eupolis, Cratinus, and Aristophanes in his mission to embarrass scoundrels in public, though he changed the form of the verse. This is a very rough comparison between two quite different literary forms, but it has stuck, partly thanks to Persius' allusion here.

     adflate a vocative pple., the sense of which is completed by *audaci . . . Cratino*, an abl. of cause. *adflate* is appropriate because all three poets are portrayed as full of passion (not to say hot air).

124   **praegrandi . . . sene** Aristophanes, though Cratinus' junior, became the top figure in the Old Comic canon and so can be evoked with this grand circumlocution. Persius implies that a learned reader can figure out the puzzle.

     palles "grows pale (with excitement) over" (+ acc.)

125   **haec** Persius' poetry

si . . . audis really "if you want to hear" or "if you have an ear for"

decoctius one of many food metaphors seen in Roman literary-critical poems, and satire in particular. This comparative form might be a true comparative, claiming Persius' work is more refined than Old Comedy, or it might simply be an intensified positive ("something rather refined").

126 **inde** "from these sources" (the comic poets); the cause of *ferveat*

vaporata . . . aure abl. of description. This refined, perceptive ear contrasts with the foolish, undiscriminating *auriculae* of Persius' targets in this poem.

mihi used in a possessive sense with *lector*

127–34 **non hic . . . do** and now the other side of the coin: the types that Persius does *not* want as readers. This satiric description is as important to Persius' self-presentation as the portrait of the discriminating reader.

127 **in** "at," "against"

128 **sordidus** the enjambment suggests that we may translate as an addendum to the previous line: "that low-life"

qui possit rel. clause of characteristic. Some scholars read this as a criticism of the person's cruelty, but *possit* may point to his *inability* to come up with any other joke.

129 **sese aliquem credens** supply *esse*

Italo . . . honore "because of his official position in an Italian town," abl. of cause explaining *supinus* ("with his head thrown back")

130 **fregerit** pf. subjunctive in the causal *quod* clause

aedilis "as an aedile," one of the magistrates in an Italian town (Arretium is modern Arezzo)

131 **abaco . . . metas** mathematicians drew their calculations and diagrams on tables covered in sand or dust; they marked points with cones

132   **scit** implying that the man thinks highly of his abilities

       paratus the pple.; takes the inf.

133   **nonaria** a woman who starts work at the ninth hour of the day; i.e., a prostitute. Persius imagines her taunting a philosopher (the bearded *sapiens* is a Roman stereotype; cf. **Juvenal 14.12**). The Cynic school practiced diatribe, like the Stoics (and satirists; cf. **Horace 1.1**), and we might readily accept that Persius would object to any mockery of a fellow philosopher. But it must be noted that the satirist has contrived this odd image himself, and forces us to imagine the silly scene. If he elicits a smile from his reader, he is having his cake and eating it too.

134   **edictum** probably a playbill from the theater (cf. Seneca *Epistle* 117.30)

       Callirhoen acc. sing. Because this is the name of the heroine of one of our earliest Greek romance novels (Chariton's *Chaereas and Callirhoe*), many scholars have been tempted to read this as a direct reference and to date the novel to Persius' lifetime. Others speculate that the name refers to a character in a mime or similarly popular genre. Persius' specifications for morning and afternoon reading seem to imply that the general public even finds reading a physical challenge. Persius' ideal reader, as described above, surrenders himself mentally and physically to reading.

✑ *Foolish prayers,* Persius *Satire* 2.1–16

This poem is wider in its scope than the first, but also a bit gentler in its criticisms. Persius here considers the human tendency to make unrealistic prayers. Throughout, people who pray for riches without adjusting their own behavior are made to seem ridiculous, even irredeemably tainted; at the same time, there are notes of pathos and even compassion in these vignettes. Persius criticizes the petitioners' attitudes and methods, but never demonizes them. This blend of perspectives is a key feature of Persius' satiric method, and makes this poem quite different from the more famous satire that imitates it, Juvenal *Satire* 10. The Juvenalian version is written on a grand scale and filled with historical and mythological examples illustrating its argument. More important, its very argument is rather different from Persius': Juvenal claims that prayers *when fulfilled* can lead to disaster. Persius' contrasting focus on unfulfilled, futile prayers allows him to explore the private feelings and the weaknesses of ordinary people rather than observing with relish their spectacular failures. Note also the physicality of his descriptions of people, which unlike the caricaturish vignettes in **Horace 1.1** makes them seem vulnerable and sad, if deeply flawed.

1   **Macrine** according to the ancient commentary, a close older friend of Persius

        numera . . . lapillo Persius seems to be imagining Macrinus marking each day with a stone, perhaps on a calendar of sorts, though this is not an attested Roman practice. A white stone would presumably indicate a particularly propitious day; *candidus* is also used in Latin to mean "frank" or "sincere," and so nicely foreshadows the praise of honest, "candid" prayers a few lines down.

2   **qui . . . apponet** rel. clause of purpose

3   **non tu** Macrinus is wise enough to pray properly; still, Persius proceeds with his lecture

        emaci abl.; "haggling"

4   **quae** n. acc. pl. denoting the content of the prayer; introduces a rel. clause of characteristic

        divis dat. governed by *committere*

5   **at . . . procerum** note the echo of **Horace *Satire* 1.1.61**, a similar but more elaborate generalization. The fut. verb here is gnomic (GL 242 N.1).

        tacita transferred epithet; it is the prayer (or the petitioner) that is silent

6   **murmurque** acc. On the double -**que**, see note on **Lucilius 1146**.

8   **mens bona ... fides** a sneaky man puts on his act in a temple

     haec refers to the quote; supply *dicit* and *verba*

     hospes another visitor to the temple, or a guest at a domestic ritual

9   **illa** the counterpart of *haec* above, referring to the next quote (thus the comparison in 8–10 has a neat chiastic structure; see GL 682)

     sub lingua we would say "under his breath"

     o si "if only"

10   **ebulliat** "pop off"

     praeclarum funus supply something like *hoc sit*. Since *funus* has several meanings, this could mean "a grand funeral" or "an excellent corpse."

11   **mihi** dat. of advantage, but can be translated with possessive sense (with *rastro*)

12   **Hercule** in an abl. absolute with *dextro* (in the sense "favorable"). Hercules, granted immortality after his death, was one of the gods the Romans associated with wealth (another is Mercury; see line 44). This prayer is more harmless than the others, if the most unrealistic.

12-13 **pupillumve ... expungam** another desired boon, and the most malicious prayer in the passage. *proximus* indicates that the ward is just ahead of the speaker in a will; *expungam* means "rub off (the list)" but has more sinister overtones as well. This speaker will remind the reader of the legacy-hunter in **Horace Satire 2.5**; Persius' ensuing description of the "mangy" heir looks like a graphic elaboration of line 45 of that poem.

14   **Nerio** dat. of advantage, but again implying possession as well. The name may be meant to recall a moneylender mentioned at Horace *Satire* 2.3.69.

     conditur the pres. implies "at this moment"

15   **ut poscas** purpose clause. Persius now addresses the shifty character directly. The variation is not unusual for this poet, but here it subtly associates Macrinus—as well as the outside

reader—with the satire's targets, as if following the "Tantalus rule" from **Horace 1.1**. Persius will not let his audience feel smug.

Tiberino in gurgite the Tiber river flowed through Rome. Rivers were often used for rituals of purification.

16   **noctem** meaning "things you've done at night"

ꙮ *Foolish prayers* (continued), Persius *Satire* 2.31–52

31   **ecce** makes the illustration more immediate and dramatic

metuens with the sense of an adj. ("superstitious"); takes an objective gen. (*divum* is the regular gen. pl. of *divus*)

cunis abl. of separation following *exemit* in 32

32   **atque** joins the two accs., whereas *-que* after *frontem* joins the two verbs

33   **infami** the middle finger was used in obscene gestures and, because of its perceived power, in apotropaic rites. The woman uses her finger to anoint the baby with saliva (pl. for sing.).

ante adv.; precedes *expiat*

34   **urentis** acc. pl.; refers to the malicious (and therefore "burning") evil eye that jealous people might direct at a fortunate neighbor. The woman who is solely obsessed with the boy's success in life is unsurprisingly distrustful of all other people.

perita cf. the note on *callidus* at **Persius 1.118**

35   **quatit** supply *puerum* as object; *manibus* is abl. of means

macram her hope is figuratively "skinny" because it is unrealistic, though the epithet also conjures the image of the tiny baby and the pathetic look of the old woman

36   **Licini** a wealthy ex-slave of Julius Caesar. The woman aims her hope at (the sense of *in* + acc.) wealth like his.

Crassi the colleague of Julius Caesar and Pompey, also famous for his enormous wealth

37 **optet generum** "desire as a son-in-law." The subjunctive is optative.

38 **rapiant** "snatch at," "scramble for"

quidquid direct object. This is a different sort of prayer than the others, with its fairy-tale quality; it does pick up the earlier images of the ground and earth (cf. *humilis . . . susurros* in line 6 and the lucky hoe in 11).

hic pron.

39 **negato** 2nd person fut. imperative (cf. **Horace Satire 2.5.29**), for added formality and drama in Persius' address to the highest god

40 **albata** the operative word: "dressed in (solemn, pious) white"

rogarit pf. subjunctive after *quamvis*

41 **poscis** note the shift to 2nd person (cf. **Horace 1.1.68–69**)

nervis . . . senectae both dats., but the first is an indirect object while the second follows the adj. *fidele*

42 **esto age** "very well then"

43 **vetuere** cf. **Lucilius 545**; this = *vetuerunt*, as scansion will reveal (note in contrast the short first *e* in *adnuere*). *veto* takes the acc. and inf. (*adnuere superos*). The image is striking: the very power of the gods is constrained by the man's unhealthy diet.

45 **da fortunare Penatis** *fortunare* usually means "make prosper," but many editors construe it intransitively here: "give (to me that) my stores prosper." The *Penates* were the gods of the household stores.

46 **da . . . fetum** perhaps not grammatically parallel to the first request: "give me a herd and offspring for my flocks"

quo, pessime, pacto the same question Horace asks Davus at *Satire* 2.7.22, showing his anger and lack of authority at the moment; Persius, by contrast, is stern and forceful

47 **tibi** dat. of disadvantage, with a hint of possession (cf. lines 11 and 14)

48   **hic** pron. Persius switches from 2nd person back to 3rd, seeming to give up on advising the man further and letting us watch him race toward his doom.

49-50   **iam . . . iam . . . iam iam** the repetition conveys excitement, perhaps tinged with growing desperation

50   **dabitur** in his excitement the man supplies no subject; understand "wealth," but a vague "it's coming to me" or "this is it" would also be suitable translations

50-51   **donec . . . suspiret** the subjunctive implies that the event is caused by the action in the main clause, and inevitable (GL 572 R.1)

51   **fundo** here the bottom of a chest or purse

        nummus a surprise, since *deceptus et exspes* in the previous line suggests an animate subject for the verb. The personification of the coin, while humorous, implicitly criticizes the man for even making his money into a "victim."

∾ *The satirist's philosophical and ethical roots, Persius Satire 5.21–51*

Persius begins his longest and most formally structured poem by conveying gratitude to his tutor, the Stoic Cornutus, for inspiring him in his examination of moral topics. He describes the training Cornutus gave him and expresses affection in a way that is highly reminiscent of Horace's poems to Maecenas. At the same time, this passage has a personal tone and striking descriptions that are unique to Persius. Note the many interesting metaphors for personal intimacy, teaching, and speech. Persius continues to use the language of bodies and body parts also seen in *Satire 2*, but here it serves as one of his striking devices for describing inner thoughts and character.

21   **secrete loquimur** recall the pretense of secrecy at the end of Persius 1; here a veneer of intimacy and private language covers a poem that will certainly be read by others

22   **excutienda** cf. the description of Horace's nose as *excussus* at **Persius 1.118**. Persius himself is concerned not with taste, but with the secrets of the heart (*praecordia*).

22-23   **nostrae ... animae** gen. with *pars*

22-25   **quanta ... ostendisse iuvat** the first of two indirect questions; the second comes in 24–25. The pf. inf. may imply that Persius feels his work is already under way.

24   **pulsa** "knock"; Persius invites Cornutus to test him even now

24-25   **dinoscere cautus . . . et** "careful at distinguishing (X) from (Y)." This describes Cornutus. The two objects of *dinoscere* are an indirect question (*quid ... crepet*) and a simple acc. (*tectoria*).

25   **solidum** an acc. of inner object after *crepet* ("sounds solid")

      pictae tectoria linguae a colorful metaphor for disingenuous speech

26   **hic** if this reading of the text is correct (some manuscripts read *hinc* or *his*), this must be adverbial and have the sense "now," "for this task"

      centenas used as if equivalent to *centum* (GL 97 N.1). The suggestion that a grand poetic subject requires multiple mouths is a commonplace that begins with Homer (see *Iliad* 2.489).

      ausim an archaic pf. subjunctive with potential sense

27   **quantum ... fixi** the indicative in this indirect question adds vividness to an already striking image

      sinuoso the adj. conjures an image of Persius' heart as a toga with deep "pockets" (cf. **Juvenal 1.88**), maintaining the aura of intimacy

28   **traham** here "ponder," "consider"

      verba resignent another purpose clause, using *ut* from the previous line. Poetry will effectively translate the private language in Persius' heart.

29   **fibra** cf. *praecordia* in line 22. While the word can be construed roughly as "heart," notice that Persius also uses the word in its concrete sense "entrails" (see 46). This satirist makes mental processes out to be a physical, even visceral, business.

30   **pavido ... mihi** dat. of interest (reference), but may be translated like an abl. of separation

custos ... purpura Persius refers to the purple-bordered *toga praetexta*, worn by boys under sixteen and thus figured here as a "guardian." It was then replaced by a white toga (see 33).

31   **bulla ... pependit** the *bulla* was a protective amulet, another sign of childhood, which was dedicated to the household gods (*Lares*) when the child reached puberty. The *Lares* were traditionally pictured in girded (tucked-up) clothing.

32   **cum blandi comites** supply *erant*

Subura abl. of place. Literary sources suggest that this busy and densely populated Roman neighborhood was best known for its large number of visible prostitutes.

33   **permisit sparsisse** supply *me*. The inf. is modified by *inpune* in 32.

umbo the fold of a garment, here standing for the garment itself (synecdoche), and personified like *purpura* in 30

34–35   **cum ... est et ... diducit** a generalization about all "restless" (*trepidas*) young men

iter ambiguum ... ramosa in compita the image evokes a story in which Hercules (a hero to the Stoics) chooses the "path" of virtue over leisure; see Xenophon's *Memorabilia* 2.1.21–33

36   **me tibi supposui ... suscipis** Cornutus became a combination of master and adoptive father (*suscipere* is similar to *tollere* as used at **Horace 2.5.46**). The switch to the pres. tense makes the story seem more immediate—and after all, the relationship between the two men is ongoing.

37   **Socratico ... sinu** Socrates is not a model for the Stoic school in particular (his pupil Plato founded the Academic school), but he does represent a dedicated teacher and friend of young men. If we translate *sinu* as "embrace" or "intimacy," we also get across a hint of Socrates' reputed affection for his

particularly attractive followers. Persius allows us to entertain this hint, since he implies that his philosophical training was a substitute for erotic adventure.

fallere sollers "skilled at escaping notice" (cf. *dinoscere cautus*, 24); Cornutus' "ruler" was not harsh but subtle

38 **intortos extendit . . . mores** there is an echo of Aristotle's *Nicomachean Ethics* 2.9, where flawed individuals are metaphorized as bent sticks needing straightening

39 **premitur . . . vincique laborat** Cornutus taught the young Persius to see the value in "pressure" and "conquest" by reason

40 **tuo ducit sub pollice** an image of teaching as working in clay, seen elsewhere in Persius (3.23–24) and in Juvenal (7.237–38). *ducit* has the sense "takes on," "assumes."

41-42 **tecum . . . noctes** evokes the long sessions dramatized in Plato's dialogues; note the repetitive and balanced structure

42 **epulis** probably dat. of purpose

decerpere cf. Horace's famous command *carpe diem* (*Odes* 1.11.8)

43 **unum** applies to both acc. nouns in the line; as the previous line also indicates, both work and leisure activity played a part in Persius' training

ambo modifies the subject

44 **verecunda . . . mensa** one of many reminders in Roman satire that "you are what you eat." The abl. expresses place.

seria a substantive

45 **hoc** explained in the acc. + inf. construction in 46

dubites potential subjunctive, with either a true or an "ideal" second person. Here the verb takes an acc. + inf.

45-51 **amborum . . . astrum** a series of astrological explanations for the bond between teacher and student, reflecting beliefs about fate and friendship and echoing Horace's address to Maecenas at *Odes* 2.17.15–24. Astrology was so popular throughout the Roman world that even philosophers acknowledged its relevance. The exact sense of Persius' explanation, however, has largely eluded modern scholars. One interpretation holds that both men were born when the constellation Gemini was rising.

46   **uno sidere duci** presumably the astrological sign

48   **tenax** i.e., "close companion of"; *veri* is a substantive

fidelibus used substantively and taken after *nata* ("meant for," "destined for")

49   **dividit in** "divides (acc. *concordia fata*) between"

duorum i.e., "us two"

50   **Saturnum** some believed this planet had a malicious power that was balanced by the benign influence of Jupiter (in myth, the father and son were at odds). Thus Persius may mean that at his and Cornutus' births the planets were positioned in such a way as to achieve this balance.

frangimus i.e., "overwhelm," "defeat"

51   **nescio . . . astrum** envision the sense as *certe est quod nescio quod astrum me tibi temperat.* Understand something like "but whatever the exact cause" preceding this. **nescio quod** is from *nescio quis*, equivalent to an indefinite pron.

temperat either in its usual sense "rule," "govern" (+ acc.) followed by a dat. of advantage, or "make (acc.) conform to (dat.)," "blend (acc.) with (dat.)"

∾ *Identifying a crisis,* Juvenal *Satire* 1.63–93

In this poem Juvenal defends his choice to write satire by cataloguing the moral and social problems of contemporary Rome, hyperbolically and in lurid detail. To the reader coming from Persius' quieter, inward-looking, and often cryptic satire, Juvenal's debut comes across as the complete opposite—an aggressive diatribe that fires off repeated rhetorical questions as if bullying the reader into agreeing with the satirist. But the reader who persists is rewarded with a dramatic and shocking picture of the world Juvenal claims to inhabit, and especially of the seamy side of Roman social behavior and customs. This is the strategy of the angry persona of *Satires* 1–6: to lure the reader in part with sensational material, and in part by implying repeatedly that the indignant response is the only correct response. Some modern scholars have proposed that Juvenal intends mainly to create a parody of extremist rhetoric and to invite his educated readers to enjoy the joke. But this view assumes a clear line between the enjoyment of parody as such and the more emotional, engaged enjoyment of the "buzz" that can come from listening to powerful rhetoric. There may not have been such a solid line in Roman intellectual culture, as there is not always one in our own. We should entertain the possibility that ancient readers—who were capable of both emotions and social prejudices—sometimes enjoyed Juvenal's brand of rage and humor in less critical and more visceral ways. At the very least, we may imagine that the satirist enjoyed putting his audience to this test. By the end of the catalogue in *Satire* 1, the reader may well accept Juvenal's assertion that satiric poetry is needed more urgently than (and is just as exciting as) grand verse dealing with remote mythological subjects (cf. 1.1–21, 51–54). The first passage below includes typical Juvenalian elements: a description of satire's subject-matter as the "hodge-podge" of human experience (with the improbable claim that the author is simply scribbling his thoughts on the spot), vignettes of excessive or criminal behavior, memorable satiric aphorisms, and a debunking version of an ancient myth. Finally, lines 87–88 hint that we are being subjected to a conventional *locus de saeculo*, or (hyperbolic) summary of the depraved present generation. Students of rhetoric were taught how to employ this commonplace as a rousing digression in the midst of a speech on a specific incident or person. But Juvenal's entire first poem amounts to a sweeping condemnation of the current age.

63   **nonne** aggressive rhetorical questions are one sign of the "angry mode"; they are scattered throughout this passage

       ceras Romans used wax tablets for writing messages, and often in Latin *cera* stands for the tablet itself; cf. **14.29**

64   **quadrivio** abl. of place. Here the satirist would have a good
      view in all directions, as well as access to passersby and gossip
      (cf. *trivium* and English "trivia").

      iam sexta cervice i.e., *iam sex cervicibus*. A team of slaves
      would shoulder the poles of a litter; this man must have re-
      cently upgraded from a team of four.

      cum . . . feratur causal *cum* clause (GL 586)

66   **multum referens de** "strongly recalling," "much like." Some
      later writers portray Horace's patron as a symbol of effemi-
      nacy and luxurious living (cf. Juvenal 12.38–39 and Seneca
      Epistle 114.4–6).

67   **falsi** a substantive here, meaning a forged or misleading doc-
      ument (e.g., a will)

67-68 **qui . . . fecerit** a causal rel. clause

68   **gemma . . . uda** a moistened seal pressed into wax authenti-
      cated a document

70   **viro . . . sitiente** abl. absolute, but the *vir* is also the implied
      indirect object of *porrectura* (from *porrigo*)

      rubetam toad's lung was an ingredient in poisons; cf. Juvenal
      6.659

71   **melior Lucusta** "a superior (version of) Lucusta," who was a
      notorious poisoner of the Neronian period (see Tacitus *An-
      nals* 12.66 and Suetonius *Nero* 33.3)

72   **per famam et populum** *per populum* is a more literal use of
      the prep., while *per famam* is almost adverbial: "with scandal"
      (*Oxford Latin Dictionary, per* 16a). Such an application of one
      word to two others in two different senses is called syllepsis.

      nigros an effect of poisoning

      efferre i.e., to burial

73-74 **aude . . . si vis esse aliquid** one of Juvenal's pithy, bitter
      aphorisms

73   **Gyaris** a small island to which some convicts were banished

      carcere the holding cell for prisoners awaiting execution

74   **probitas . . . alget** another famous aphorism. A literal translation produces the best effect: *probitas* transforms from an abstraction to a (pathetic) personification.

75   **debent** the subject is criminals in high places; *criminibus* (here in the sense of profitable "crimes") is the indirect object

      hortos the pl. denotes a large garden of the sort maintained by the wealthy (cf. the sing. at **3.228**)

76   **stantem extra pocula** refers to a relief on a goblet or set of goblets (cf. **3.205**). The pl. *pocula* suits the metrical scheme; for consistency it may be translated as sing., or *caprum* as pl.

77-78 **quem . . . quem** repetition for effect, or anaphora. The phrasing of this question plays up Juvenal's self-perception as a victim.

77   **nurus** gen. sing.

78   **praetextatus** i.e., very young. Latin *adulter* refers to a male lover of a married woman, *adultera* (cf. Juvenal 14.25) to an unfaithful married woman.

79   **si natura . . . versum** another famous epigram, which misleadingly suggests that this poem has emerged fully formed from the satirist's head, shaped by emotion alone. Juvenal has already undercut this claim in the poem's introduction, where he suggests (lines 15–17) that his prior training in rhetoric is suitable background for the present literary endeavor.

      versum generalizing sing.; note the change to pl. in the next line

80   **qualemcumque . . . Cluvienus** The wording in the second half of the line is economical (brachylogy): understand *quales versus ego facio vel Cluvienus facit*. This is another (disingenuous) caveat about Juvenal's abilities. Cluvienus, presumably a bad poet, is not mentioned in any other source.

81-84 **ex quo . . . puellas** *ex quo* has temporal sense ("ever since"), and introduces the story of Deucalion, Pyrrha, and the cataclysmic flood sent by Jupiter, which Ovid narrates at *Metamorphoses* 1.262–415. Because of their piety, Deucalion and

Pyrrha survived the great flood, and with help from an oracle, created a new race of humans from rocks. Even Juvenal's brief account conjures Ovid's wonderful images of the world turned upside down, and this contributes to the quasi-epic grandeur of this programmatic poem.

81 **nimbis tollentibus** abl. absolute; the pple. takes *aequor* (acc.) as a direct object

82 **navigio** abl. of means

83 **mollia** used proleptically or predicatively (see note on **Horace 1.4.119**); i.e., the rocks grew soft as they grew warm

84 **nudas** inevitable, given the circumstances; still, this word gives a humorously salacious color to the scene

85–86 **quidquid agunt . . . libelli est** a summary of Juvenal's first book (a *libellus* was a single scroll). The sweeping claim is misleading—Juvenal's specific interest is the vices of Roman society—but it intriguingly suggests that the satirist is more fascinated than appalled by human nature.

85 **agunt** i.e., "have done and still do" since the flood

86 **farrago** mixed cattle fodder; the word both conveys the miscellaneous quality of satire, and hints at the prominence of food and the body as subjects. The sing. form is equated with the list of human doings.

87 **uberior** supply *fuit umquam*

88 **maior** a predicate adj. (cf. 83), but can be translated adverbially

avaritiae . . . sinus Juvenal now focuses on one vice. The image is that of a capacious pocket or fold in a toga.

88–89 **alea . . . animos** another specific complaint. The missing verb is either "has produced" (in men who gamble) or "has taken on" (personifying the dice).

89 **neque enim** "for example . . . not" or "as a matter of fact . . . not"

89–92 **neque enim . . . armigero** the impers. passives (*itur, luditur*) and the martial imagery evoke grand epic, but the content is modern and debased

89   **loculis comitantibus** parallels *posita . . . arca* in the next line.
      loculi are too small for the modern gambler.

91-92 **dispensatore . . . armigero** abl. absolute of two nouns; as
      always when translating this type, supply "as" between the
      nouns. The ordinary *dispensator* is absurdly elevated to the
      status of a hero's squire.

92   **simplex** ambiguous; this could mean "ordinary" or "tradi-
      tional," with the implied answer "no," or it could have adver-
      bial sense ("simply madness") with the emphasis on *furor* and
      the expected answer "yes"

      sestertia property totaling 400 *sestertia* conferred eques-
      trian status on the owner, so the amount Juvenal names is
      outrageous

93   **et** "and yet"; cf. **Horace 1.1.71**

      reddere either "duly give," noting the master's responsibil-
      ity if the slave was visibly *horrens*, or "give back" because the
      slave had loaned the tunic as gambling collateral. The image
      echoes Persius 1.54, where a *comes* is the shivering party.

❧ *Identifying a crisis* (continued), Juvenal *Satire* 1.135–46

Toward the end of the poem, Juvenal takes a page from his satiric
predecessors and focuses on greed and its repercussions. In this ex-
cerpt, he describes a miserly rich man who ignores the needs of his
dependent clients. The offender is a monster who drives the satirist
to new heights of indignation. It turns out, however, that justice can
come even in Juvenal's Rome, albeit slowly and indirectly. The rich
man pays the ultimate price for his behavior, and is mocked.

135   **optima** a substantive

      vorabit the lines just before this narrate the morning routine
      of clients and patrons; the fut. verb looks ahead to the patron's
      evening

136   **rex** a term sometimes applied to patrons (Horace *Epistle* 1.17.43, Juv. 5.14)

       horum clients who have been denied dinner invitations in the previous lines (hence the *vacui* couches)

       tantum adv.

137-38 **nam de . . . mensa** a troublesome passage for scholars. Most think it means that even if a rich man sets only one table (*mensa*, denoting a table in use) of the many fine round tables (*orbes*, denoting tables as furniture) in his collection, his opulent meal costs the equivalent of other men's entire estates.

138   **comedunt** like *vorabit*, suggests a more intense (and less civilized) kind of consumption than *edunt* would; in this case it is appropriate, since the object is *patrimonia*. The subject has become pl.: understand "rich patrons."

139   **parasitus** the word (Greek for "by the table") refers to a lackey who accompanies a patron to meals and provides entertainment and flattery—a type character featured throughout Roman comic and satiric literature. Juvenal is joking that even this "civilized" practice will die out as patrons grow stingier and more antisocial.

139-40 **sed quis . . . luxuriae sordes** could a parasite or client even stand to perform his role in such circumstances? "The filth/meanness of luxury" is a wonderful Juvenalian oxymoron, although *luxuria* had long had negative associations for Roman moralists.

141   **animal** a nice role-reversal joke, if this refers to the diner rather than the (pl.) boars

142-44 **poena tamen . . . senectus** Juvenal has borrowed this anecdote from a longer passage in Persius (3.98–106), where a gourmand rejects his doctor's advice and takes a fatal hot bath directly after eating (an unwise practice, according to some ancient medical writers). There is also an echo of the idea at **Horace 1.4.126–27**. Note also the shift to direct address (cf. **Persius 2.41**).

142   **amictus** acc. pl.

143   **portas** "lug (inside you)"

144   **mortes** poetic pl.; supply *veniunt*

       intestata senectus the adj. either means "without heirs" (be-
       cause this hateful man has alienated even them) or "without
       a will" (because death comes so suddenly). Again the theme
       of wills and heirs finds its way into satire. At *Satire* 3.272–75,
       Juvenal jokes that it is wise to make a will before heading out
       for the evening, given the many physical dangers of the city.

145   **tristis** nom. sing. f.

       per cunctas . . . cenas appropriate, since the man perverted
       the traditional *cena* in life

146   **plaudendum** modifies *funus* (here "funeral procession") and
       looks to the dat. of agent, *iratis . . . amicis* (here most certainly
       "clients," the man's victims in life). *plaudendum* makes a good
       joke; a death ought to be described as *plangendum*. Cf. **Per-
       sius 2.10**, "*praeclarum funus!*"

∾ *Trials of the urban poor,* Juvenal *Satire* 3.190–231

Throughout most of this poem, the long centerpiece of Juvenal's first
book, a man named Umbricius is speaking. On the verge of a move
to the country, he is explaining (ostensibly to his friend the satirist)
why he feels compelled to leave Rome. Umbricius identifies himself—
rather sanctimoniously—as a virtuous and struggling urban pauper
who cannot survive in a social system that rewards only wealth, social
connections, and unscrupulous ambition. In his bitter tirade, he criss-
crosses the busy city again and again to point to typical episodes that
illustrate the pauper's endless plight and the unfair privileges of the
wealthy. Throughout the poem, Umbricius undercuts his own claims
of virtue and frugality with his obvious resentment, his suspiciously
polished tirade, and his ability to turn the pauper's saga into (albeit
painful) entertainment. Juvenal seems to have created these cracks
in this character's presentation deliberately, much as he does with his

own over-the-top tirades and morally inconsistent commentary in other *Satires*. This makes it possible for the reader to view Umbricius as an alter ego for the satirist, created to expose the imperfections of the self-appointed moralist, and hence to adopt a somewhat detached view of his bitter tirade. All the same, even a detached reader will occasionally be pushed to feel discomfort or sympathy by Umbricius' jarring mixture of anger, humor, and descriptions of real inequity or suffering. The passage below illustrates the poem's theme in a nutshell: it recounts the burning of a poor man's apartment building and the aftermath, comparing it with the scenario of a disaster that befalls a rich household. The pair of scenes is cleverly balanced to bring out the social and economic chasm between the two victims.

190-92 **Praeneste . . . Volsiniis . . . Gabiis . . . Tiburis** towns in Latium and Etruria (see map)

190 **aut timuit** supply *umquam*

gelida towns at higher elevations make ideal retreats during hot Italian summers

191 **positis nemorosa inter iuga** Volsinii was situated in a rugged region of Etruria

192 **simplicibus** a misleading epithet; these locales were the sites of plenty of luxurious retreats for the well-off, a fact that undercuts Umbricius' portrayal of country life as old-fashioned and frugal

proni Tibur was also situated on a hill; hence "spread out, face-down" as if in relaxation

arce abl. of place

193 **nos** i.e., "but we back in Rome"

194 **magna parte** abl. of specification. *sui* may seem superfluous, but it is acceptable in the Latin expression.

sic i.e., *tenui tibicine fultam*. The analogy has both a serious and a comic side.

labentibus used substantively to indicate the buildings, their occupants, or both

196 **securos** part of the indirect command; may be translated adverbially and after *dormire*. Umbricius complains later in the poem that it is hard to sleep in Rome; this recalls the satirist's own remark at **1.77**.

iubet with the same sense as in *iubere valere* at **Horace 1.1.63**

197-98 **nulla . . . metus** supply *sunt*; Juvenal again refers to the countryside

198 **nocte** abl. of time

198-99 **iam . . . fumant** the generalization transforms into a vivid narrative, unfolding in "real time" with each instance of *iam* (cf. **Persius 2.50–51**)

198 **transfert** i.e., "carries out to safety"

199 **Ucalegon** in Vergil's *Aeneid*, a Trojan whose house burns during the sack of Troy (2.311). In Homer's *Iliad*, he is a Trojan elder (3.148). The epic allusion lends grandeur to Juvenal's account of the fire, while the name itself (Greek for "uncaring") underscores his neighbor's helplessness.

tabulata . . . tertia the poor man presumably lives on the highest, least comfortable, and least safe storey of his apartment building. Several buildings of this kind are partially preserved at Ostia (Rome's port city) and Herculaneum (see, e.g., http://www.vroma.org/images/mcmanus_images/apartmentbldg2.jpg).

199-200 **tibi . . . tu nescis** with this brief lapse into direct address, Umbricius/Juvenal forces the reader to experience the scene from inside the burning building—and in the pauper's shoes

200 **trepidatur** an impers. pass. that aptly suggests general panic

201 **ultimus ardebit** the poor man (now back in 3rd person) is "the last to burn"—due to ignorance, not luck

202 **molles ubi reddunt ova columbae** the image could be solemn and idyllic on its own, but Juvenal uses it to emphasize the tenant's dehumanizing living situation

203 **Cordo** dat. of possession with *erat*. This is a common cognomen, but Juvenal probably invented this character.

Procula minor i.e., "too small for Procula," who must have been a small woman known to Juvenal's original audience

204   **ornamentum** in apposition to *urceoli* (line 203). The possessions listed are all small (note *parvulus*) imitations of a rich man's goods.

abaci the gen. is better translated with "for" than with "of"

nec non a common poetic circumlocution, here intensified by *et*

infra i.e., stowed below the table, presumably on a shelf or hook

205   **sub eodem marmore** probably corrupted text, and difficult to interpret. It might mean "made from the same piece of marble," or the original text may have read (as some commentators believe) *sub eo de marmore.* If this is still part of the description of the *cantharus*, Juvenal must be referring to a carving of Chiron on its side below the rim. Centaurs are often portrayed drinking at symposia or dinners.

206   **iam(que)** modifying *vetus*

Graecos . . . libellos scrolls of Greek poetry, as indicated by *carmina* in 207

207   **divina** many poets (though almost never satiric poets) claim to be aided by deities. The line is "golden" (see Introduction)— a delightfully ironic touch, considering the subject.

opici a word Italian Greeks used by to describe their non–Greek-speaking neighbors. This application to the destructive mice is therefore quite precise. The line itself descends neatly from sublimity to chewing rodents, and suggests that Cordus' books were doomed even before the fire.

208–9   **illud . . . nihil** "he lost that whole 'nothing' of his, poor fellow"

210   **quod** "the fact that"

nudum et . . . rogantem modifying Cordus

211   **hospitio tectoque** i.e., "hospitality consisting of a roof" (hendiadys; GL 698)

212   **Asturici** unknown; presumably a prominent man. If 212–22 describe a single incident, he may be equated with or related to Persicus in line 221.

212-13 **horrida mater, pullati proceres** supply *est* and *sunt*. The sing. *mater* is generalizing: "the matrons of the city."

213 **differt vadimonia** i.e., postpones legal business. Praetors oversaw the courts.

215 **ardet** the subject is again *domus Asturici*

qui . . . donet a rel. clause of purpose. Now the previous list of the pauper's possessions—lost in one fell swoop—will be neatly balanced by this this description of the rich man's empty lot rapidly filling up with new items. The forms of *hic* in the next five lines point to different individuals.

marmora building blocks rather than statues, which arrive shortly thereafter

217 **Euphranoris et Polycliti** renowned Greek artists of the fifth and fourth centuries BCE

218 **Asianorum . . . ornamenta deorum** cf. the poor man's humble *ornamentum* (line 204). Statues and other artworks from temples in Greece and Asia (the name of the Roman province south of the Black Sea) were prized by many wealthy Romans

219 **hic . . . Minervam** while Cordus loses his old scrolls, the rich man gains a smart new library, complete with bookcases and a statue of the goddess of crafts and learning

220 **modium** suggests the silver is in the form of plate, which was measured not counted

meliora ac plura i.e., "better and more numerous than what he lost"

reponit "acquires as replacements"

221 **Persicus** see note on line 212. The name suggests luxurious tastes.

orborum lautissimus a clever oxymoron. Persicus must be one of the much-courted *orbi*, like those described in **Horace 2.5**.

222 **tamquam . . . incenderit** unlike in **Horace 1.1.71**, this *tamquam* introduces an assertion that may be well founded

223 **circensibus** the quintessential feature of the city as Juvenal portrays it, a scene of crowds, noise, and posturing

optima "very nice"

223-24   **Sorae . . . Fabrateriae . . . Frusinone** Juvenal turns his attention back to small towns in Latium (see map)

224   **paratur** "can be rented"

225   **quanti** a gen. of value; the whole line expresses the price of the *domus* in 224

nunc i.e., in Rome. Americans talk the same way about New York apartments.

226   **hortulus** a small kitchen-garden (contrast the *horti* of Juv. 1.75)

hic the adv., referring to the country

movendus *moveo* here has the sense "engage," "draw from." A shallow well means less work for the owner.

227   **tenuis plantas** delicate seedlings, not runty plants, but still reflecting the owner's small means

228   **vive** a direct recommendation to the audience

bidentis objective gen. with *amans*; a humorous image

229   **centum** modifying *Pythagoreis*, a dat. pl. and the indirect object of *dare*. Pythagoreans were vegetarians. The image of the modest garden is traditionally associated with philosophy (often specifically with Epicurus, whose school grounds included a not-so-modest garden).

230   **est aliquid** "it means something"; the subject is *fecisse* (line 231). Contrast this with the need to commit crimes in order to be *aliquid* in Rome (1.74).

231   **unius . . . lacertae** the concluding line is neatly framed by the adj. and noun

sese the object of *fecisse*; *dominum* is predicative, and denotes ownership as well as control

lacertae humble "livestock," actually plentiful in the Italian countryside!

∾ Unchaste women on display, Juvenal *Satire* 6.60–102

Juvenal's longest poem, an entire "book" unto itself (book 2), is addressed to a man who is looking for a wife. The satirist argues against this plan, providing dozens of lurid illustrations of the inconveniences of marriage, and specifically of the depravity of modern women. His views of women are even more reactionary than those of other Roman moralists who distrust women's nature and rail against any loosening of traditional restrictions on their behavior (e.g., Cato the Elder as portrayed by Livy). The satirist is also rather prurient for a moralist; he becomes a pornographer of sorts when he dwells on women's salacious behavior and secret activities. Finally, he is not averse to making jokes at the expense of women's "victims," their frustrated or deceived husbands. Thus, like the other "angry poems" of Juvenal, *Satire* 6 aims to pull the reader in different directions: toward agreement with the aggressive speaker, but also toward superior amusement at his warped views; toward sympathy with the wives' male "victims," but also sometimes with the wives themselves (always shrewder than their spouses). The substance of the satirist's claims is similarly complicated. Scholars have cautiously consulted the poem for evidence about the lives and pursuits of real Roman women, though they must at the same time always consider the distorting lens of Juvenal's angry and chauvinistic persona. The passage below begins Juvenal's series of scandalous tales. In an allusion to Ovid's *Art of Love* book 1, where the love poet urges his reader to look for mates in public places, Juvenal points to the theater seats as a particularly revealing site of women's bad behavior. We learn that women's love of the theater derives from their lust for actors. Juvenal goes on to relate examples of brazen adultery.

60   **porticibus** arcades, perfect for strolling and people-watching

61   **spectacula** the tiered seats in the theater or amphitheater; as Ovid famously writes in book 1 of his *Art of Love*, this is another fine place to survey potential mates

62   **quod . . . ames . . . possis** cf. Ovid *Art of Love* 1.91–92: *illic in-venies quod ames, quod ludere possis / quodque semel tangas, quodque tenere velis.* Like Ovid, Juvenal denotes the woman with a neuter *quod* in his rel. clauses; the clauses express characteristic. The order of the two clauses reverses the logical order (*hysteron proteron*, "the latter earlier," B 374.7).

63   **chironomon . . . Bathyllo** start translation with the abl. absolute, and note that *saltante* has an acc. of inner object ("dancing [the part of] Leda"). Leda was the mother of Helen in Greek mythology; she was impregnated by Zeus in the form of a swan.

      chironomon a Greek adj. (here in acc. sing.) meaning "with moving hands," "gesticulating," i.e., acting a part in pantomime, an immensely popular theatrical genre involving music and dance. The adj. strictly modifies *Ledam* ("the Leda in the pantomime") but really serves to describe Bathyllus.

      Bathyllo the name of a famous dancer of Augustus' time; others may have adopted this name later. The names of performers in this passage all seem to be traditional professional names; the names of the women in the audience also seem generic and invented. Nevertheless, Juvenal's use of names makes his anecdotes more vivid and even gives them a veneer of historical accuracy.

65   **sicut . . . longum** some editors bracket this line as a likely interpolation by a later scribe. The proper punctuation and sense are not clear, and the line inelegantly unpacks the succinct *gannit* in the previous line.

66   **rustica** sc. "although she is"

      Thymele the name of a mime-actress at **8.197**; if that is the case here, the line means that even a performer of fairly racy mimes will find this dance eye-opening

67   **recondita** the pple. may be translated as a verb preceding *cessant* (cf. **Horace 1.1.42**)

69   **a plebeis longe** supply *absunt*. There were no games featuring
     performances between the *ludi plebeii* (held in November in
     honor of Jupiter) and the *ludi Megalenses* or *Megalesia* (held in
     April for the goddess Cybele).

     tristes modifies *aliae* (line 67)

70   **personam ... thyrsumque ... et subligar** all theatrical props:
     the actor's mask, the staff held by bacchic revelers in a chorus,
     and the loincloth worn beneath costumes

     tenent "cling to," "handle"

71   **exodio ... Atellanae** an Atellan farce was a short comic piece,
     thought to have originated in Campania (see map) and often
     performed after more serious plays as a finale (*exodium*; the abl.
     here expresses either means or time). Some were tragic paro-
     dies; hence the mention of Autonoe (line 72; gen. sing. modi-
     fied by *Atellanae*), an aunt of the Theban king Pentheus.

Fig. 5. Terracotta group of two women conversing (Asia Minor, Hellenistic period).

72   **Aelia pauper** not only high-class women are susceptible to frivolous obsessions

73   **his . . . sunt quae** referring to two types of women

      magno "for a high price"; abl. of price. Access to famous actors is not free.

      fibula part of a kind of chastity belt for singers; sexual activity was believed to be detrimental to the voice (cf. *cantare vetent* in the next line)

75   **Quintilianus** the famous rhetorician, active in the second half of the first century CE and, incidentally, the author of a treatise on rhetoric that helps us understand Juvenal's own techniques better. At line 280 of this satire, Juvenal writes that a woman embroiled in an argument with her husband can profitably call on Quintilian for inspiration.

76   **accipis** introduces a hypothetical scenario, so may be translated as "suppose you take . . ."

76–77 **de qua . . . fiat** rel. clause of purpose

      citharoedus . . . choraules musicians who played the lute (Greek *cithara*) and flute (Greek *aule*)

78   **pulpita** perhaps referring to temporary seats lined up beside festival processions

79   **grandi** "abundant"; Juvenal now refers to a private celebration

80   **testudineo . . . conopeo** indirect object. A *conopeum* (originally a Greek word, and cf. English "canopy") designates a mosquito net or (as here) a grand bed fitted with one.

      Lentule an aristocratic *cognomen*, invoked for the contrast with the baby's real father. This is a case of apostrophe (cf. **Persius 1.115**).

81   **Euryalum** a gladiator (unknown) of the class called *murmillones* (these wore Gallic armor and a helmet with a fish emblem)

      exprimat "give the impression of," i.e., "look strikingly like," + acc.

82-94 **nupta senatori . . . mare** a long tale, presented as a historical episode (although the story is not known from other sources)

82 **ludum** here referring to a company of gladiators

83-84 **Pharon . . . Nilum . . . Lagi . . . Canopo** the sights of Egypt

84 **prodigia et mores** hendiadys, with the sense of *prodigiosos mores.* Juvenal elevates Eppia's behavior to a portent threatening national interests (*prodigia* were matters of state concern). In Juvenal's day, Canopus was famous for the pleasures it offered visiting Romans and Greeks.

urbis gen.; referring to Rome and modifying *prodigia et mores*

85 **domus** gen. sing.; it and the two gens. that follow all go with *immemor*

87 **utque magis stupeas** parenthetical, introducing the ironic climax of the list of things Eppia left behind. The second person is generalizing.

ludos here referring to shows, and recalling the theme of lines 60–75

88 **pluma** abl. with *in*

89 **parvula** "as a little girl"; cf. *puerum* at **Horace 1.4.121**

90 **contempsit . . . olim** "think nothing of"; a neat line, with its repetition of the verb and abrupt shift to a harsher tone. *famam* may be translated "as for her reputation . . ."

pelagus acc.

91 **cuius** with *iactura*; antecedent is *famam*

molles . . . cathedras the cushioned chairs of aristocratic women

92-94 **Tyrrhenos . . . mare** a comic shift to the scene on Eppia's boat

92 **late** modifies the pple.

94 **mutandum . . . esset mare** i.e., Eppia had to pass through several seas and straits

95 **ratio** with *pericli* (= *periculi*). Juvenal now generalizes from the Eppia episode.

97   **fortem . . . audent** aphoristic; cf. the similar pithy expression
       in 100

99   **sentina gravis** supply *est*

       summus vertitur aer so it seems to the sick woman. One
       might suspect she is pretending, but *illa maritum convomit*
       (lines 100–101) seems to settle the matter. *aer,* a word bor-
       rowed from Greek, is dissyllabic and makes up the last foot in
       the line. The jarring rhythm produced with this composition
       may be intended to simulate a rough sea journey.

100   **illa** the woman in 98; the other type *quae moechum sequitur*
       reappears in *haec* (line 101)

∾ *The scandal of performing nobles,* Juvenal *Satire* 8.183–99

The eighth *Satire* (the second poem of Juvenal's third book) condemns members of the Roman nobility who boast of their ancestors' virtues while practicing vices themselves. While this is one of
Juvenal's more "historical" *Satires* in its reference to real events and
noble families, it should be noted that most of the anecdotes come
from earlier eras, from the infancy of the Roman Republic to the
Julio-Claudian and Flavian periods. The decline of morality among
the aristocracy was a well-worn theme in literature and rhetoric, a
variation on the broader *locus de saeculo* exemplified in **Satire 1**. Juvenal's treatment here is original, packed with allusions to Republican and Imperial literary works and tinged with a sneering irony
that contrasts with his earlier "indignant" mode. He highlights some
nobles' abuse of public office, and others' sordid erotic adventures.
The traditional two-part strategy of Roman moralistic discourse is
to present both positive and negative models ("exempla"; cf. Tantalus in **Horace 1.1**) that illustrate, respectively, the fruits of virtue
and the costs of vice. This practice was central to Roman education
and is seen throughout literature, even the irreverent genre of satire.
Overall, however, Juvenal shows much more interest in the negative than the positive, undermining his performance as a moralist

but creating much space for humorous criticism. In the following selections, the satirist focuses on a kind of transgression that Roman moralists found particularly troubling. He condemns certain members of the nobility for being willing to perform on stage and in the arena, despite the scandal such performances incurred. Professional actors and gladiators were typically slaves or former slaves, and in the eyes of the law they were categorized with prostitutes (evidently because all such workers used their bodies to give pleasure to the public). Nevertheless, a number of cases of the "noble mime" are cited in ancient accounts. Juvenal refers to some examples that cannot be verified, but that are obviously meant to represent shocking perversion of tradition.

183-84   **quid si . . . supersint** this is an elaborate rhetorical transition from one topic to another. The debauched nobles Juvenal has just been describing may be *foedi* and *pudendi*, but, he claims, there are none worse than the group he has in mind to treat next.

quid si . . . utimur "how about if I use," or more loosely to bring the sense of outrage across: "would you believe I can use." The "royal we" in the verb form is a common rhetorical device. As usual, *utor* takes an abl.

185   **consumptis opibus** abl. absolute, indicating the cause of what comes next

Damasippe apostrophe. If Juvenal has a particular individual from recent history in mind, we do not know of him from other sources.

185-86   **vocem . . . locasti sipario** "you hired your voice to the stage" (*sipario* is metonymic). *locasti* = *locavisti*.

186   **clamosum** describes the fast-paced action and music of the mime (see note on **Horace 2.7.59–61**), in this case a ghost story by Catullus (not the famous poet but a writer of the mid-first century CE). Plautus based his *Mostellaria* ("The Haunted House") on a Greek original called *Phasma* ("ghost").

ageres ut *ageres* goes inside the purpose clause

187   **Laureolum** a fugitive slave (hence *velox*) or bandit in a mime, who was "crucified" on stage

Lentulus not necessarily the same man mentioned at **6.80**, but Juvenal's point is the same: a member of the aristocracy has been disgraced

188   **iudice me** abl. absolute, meaning "in my opinion"

189   **populo** denoting the audience, which according to Juvenal shares the guilt

frons durior the noun is often used to mean "brazenness" (cf. English "cheek"); thus the phrase means "greater shamelessness," though the ideal translation will find a way to bring out the metaphor of "hardness"

190-92 **triscurria . . . planipedes . . . alapas** references to the typical behavior and appearance of characters in mime. The coinage *triscurria* probably means "triple-buffonery" (*tris* + *scurra*), *planipedes* is "barefoot" (like mime actors), *alapae* are "whacks" (frequently given to the stock character the *stupidus*; see line 197)

190   **patriciorum** used substantively

191-92 **Fabios . . . Mamercorum** old and distinguished *gentes* (clans). The historian Dio Cassius writes that Nero sent some members of the Fabian *gens* onto the stage by Nero (*History of Rome* 61.17.4). We have no similar evidence on the Mamerci, but the association of their name with the stage carries shock value.

192   **quanti** gen. of value; performers got a fee. The word goes inside the indirect question introduced by *quid refert* (193).

sua funera if Juvenal is still thinking specifically of theatrical performances, he probably means the metaphorical "deaths" of noble reputations. Another interpretation is that Juvenal is alluding to performances of deaths such as Laureolus' (187).

193   **nullo cogente Nerone** concessive abl. absolute. Generous in sponsoring public spectacles (and to the consternation of traditionalists, an ambitious actor himself; see lines 215–30),

Nero used such events as opportunities to turn men from noble families into performers. He is said to have lured hundreds of impoverished aristocrats onto the stage by offering lavish compensation, and even to have paid some to fight in the arena. These men complied because they were desperate, or because they saw Nero's "offers" as orders (see Tacitus *Annals* 14.14.5 and Suetonius *Nero* 12). Juvenal is evidently referring to later cases here, but he will return to the special case of Nero in the next passage.

194   **dubitant** note the special meaning of "hesitate" with the inf.

    celsi praetoris since the time of Augustus, praetors had the duty of organizing public shows, and sat in a special elevated box to watch

    ludis abl. of time (cf. *munere*, **Lucilius 172**)

195-96 **finge . . . satius** Juvenal sets up a hypothetical dilemma to illustrate the skewed priorities of the modern nobility

195   **finge** "imagine" (+ acc. and inf.)

    inde . . . hinc "on one side . . . on another"; indicating alternative fates, both extreme

    gladios . . . pulpita i.e., execution (or perhaps honorable death in combat) or a stint as an actor. For the Roman of integrity, the choice is obvious, but we can guess what the depraved nobles will choose (hinted at by *tamen* in 195).

196   **quid** Juvenal uses this in place of *utrum*. Sc. *est* or *sit*.

    exhorruit with the pf., Juvenal gestures to right-thinking Romans throughout history—at least until recently

    ut sit result clause; *sit* has the sense "would prefer to become"

197   **zelotypus** the jealous husband (of *Thymeles*, gen. sing.), a stock character in mime

    stupidi another stock role; someone who is deceived and abused for laughs

    collega the term is usually applied to political colleagues; the use is ironic here

198   **res haut mira** supply *est* and take *mimus nobilis* as the subject

     tamen i.e., despite what traditional morality dictates. This sentence is one of Juvenal's famous epigrams; we see the satirist, more emotionally detached than in the earlier books, resigning himself to reality.

     citharoedo principe abl. absolute, referring to Nero

∽ The scandal of performing nobles (continued), Juvenal *Satire* 8.215–30

At the end of the last passage, Juvenal placed the blame for the current phenomenon of the "noble mime" on the emperor Nero. This is not because Nero, long dead, is still somehow forcing others to degrade themselves on stage (cf. **193**); it is because he set an example that others follow of their own accord. Nero defied convention to show off his talents on a well-publicized tour of Greek festivals. Here the late emperor becomes Juvenal's focus and target—a "noble mime" who needs a lecture himself. Juvenal goes so far as to claim that Nero's obsession with theater and his famous performances were the worst aspects of his reign; this is a good illustration of the ironic wit that has displaced the satirist's earlier moral indignation. The passage ends with an address to Nero, in which Juvenal highlights the emperor's perversion of ancient customs. The apostrophe in combination with the moral theme reminds us that Juvenal's rhetorical training included mock-speeches to historical figures on their moral or political obligations (cf. *Satire* 1.15–17).

215-16   **par . . . dissimilem** Juvenal has just been referring to Nero's crimes against his own family (and will again in this passage)

215   **Agamemnonidae** gen. sing.; the allusion is the myth of Orestes, who murdered his mother Clytemnestra (cf. Aeschylus' *Oresteia* and numerous other Greek and Roman treatments of the story). The comparison is apt not just because Nero arranged the murder of his own mother Agrippina, but also because he loved to play dramatic parts.

causa . . . rem "cause" and "case," respectively. Orestes' revenge on his mother, because it created a unique moral and legal dilemma, was a common topic in declamatory exercises (see Quintilian *Education of the Orator* 7.4.8).

216 **ille** Orestes, the subject up through line 221

217 **media inter pocula** elaborating on *caesi*. This version of the story is closer to Homer's account at *Odyssey* 11.405–26 than Aeschylus' in his play *Agamemnon*, where the king is murdered in his bath.

217-20 **sed nec . . . miscuit** Juvenal alludes to notorious acts of Nero. The emperor ordered the deaths of two daughters of his adoptive father Claudia, Antonia and Octavia; the latter had also been his wife. He poisoned Claudius' son Britannicus, among others (see Suetonius *Nero* 35 for a list, and cf. Juvenal's mention of his hired poisoner at **1.71**).

219 **coniugii** "wife." Orestes married the daughter of Helen.

220-21 **in scaena . . . non scripsit** these last two "crimes"—framed in this position as the most heinous of all—are Juvenal's bathetic punch-line, an example of *para prosdokian* ("violated expectation," or surprise ending). We might have expected a reference to other murders. Some editors read an acc. *Oresten* at the end of 220 to get an even wittier climax: "he never sang (played) the part of Orestes on stage" (cf. **6.63** and **8.186**).

221 **Troica** Nero was a poet as well as a performer, although Tacitus claims he hired help for himself (see note on **Persius 1.121**).

221-23 **quid . . . debuit ulcisci . . . quod . . . fecit** "what act committed by Nero did Verginius et al. need to avenge more?"

221-22 **Verginius . . . aut cum Vindice Galba** military commanders in the provinces who played major roles in Nero's downfall. Vindex led a revolt that put the emperor to flight and prompted his suicide; Verginius quelled the rebellion and was encouraged to claim the title of emperor himself, but it was Galba who succeeded Nero. With *cum Vindice* Juvenal avoids simply using three nominatives (cf. **Persius 1.123–24**).

223   **saeva crudaque tyrannide** abl. of time

224   **generosi** a reminder of the poem's main theme

artes Vergil memorably uses this word to denote the particularly Roman practices of war, government, and law, contrasting Rome with the more "artistic" Greece (*Aeneid* 6.847–53). Nero, of course, seems to have reverted to the Greek model (cf. 225–26 below, on his tour of Greek festivals), and Juvenal could be alluding to the Vergilian passage in order to underscore the emperor's transgression.

225-26 **gaudentis . . . prostitui** modifies *principis* in 224. *gaudeo* may take an inf.; if that is the case here, *foedo cantu* may be taken as an abl. of means. *prostituo* often has the specific sense of its English cognate.

225   **peregrina** specifically, Greek; Nero toured the Greek games in 66–67 CE

226   **apium** one kind of crown given to victors in Greek contests

227   **maiorum . . . vocis** Roman nobles in the Republican and early Imperial periods decorated statues of their ancestors (*effigies*) with emblems of their own military and political successes (*Satire* 8 begins with a description of these statues, which amounts to a parade of positive exempla). Juvenal cynically suggests that the "noble mimes" adjust the practice to commemorate their disgraceful public acts.

228   **Domiti** an ancestor of Nero, whose name before his adoption into the Julian family was L. Domitius Ahenobarbus

228-29 **Thyestae . . . Antigones . . . Melanippes** all Greek gen. sings., referring to famous tragic roles. Thyestes was tricked by his brother, whose wife he had seduced, into eating his own children. Antigone was put to death for burying her brother in defiance of a royal decree. Melanippe was imprisoned while her children were persecuted. Note that Juvenal has been referring to tragic subjects in the Nero passage, in contrast to the list of comic roles in the previous selection. No doubt Juvenal is mocking Nero for favoring female roles and (appropriately for this philandering emperor) the role of an adulterer. But the tragic examples also suggest a darker satiric perspective on the debasement of the aristocracy in general.

229   **syrma** the robe worn by tragic actors (a Greek acc. sing. here)

230   **marmoreo ... colosso** evidently not the most famous "Colossus" of Nero, which was made of brass

∾ *The good old days,* Juvenal *Satire* 13.38–70

Satire 13 is addressed to a man named Calvinus who has been defrauded of a loan. It is the first poem of Juvenal's fifth and final book, and like **Satire** 8, it exhibits a very different satiric mode from the "angry style" of books 1 and 2. In this case, the differences are even more striking, since the poem is concerned with the kind of criminal incident that aroused indignation in the angry satirist. It is Calvinus who feels the indignation here, while the cynical satirist criticizes and even mocks his response. Juvenal chides Calvinus for his naive expectations and emotions. He elaborates on his own worldview in the passage below, where he imagines a long-lost innocent age and asserts that its customs have long since died out. This is a variation on the *locus de saeculo* (cf. the first selection from **Satire** 1)—here not a speech condemning the present generation, but a nostalgic portrait of a lost time. Besides making fun of his addressee's moral naïveté, Juvenal takes the idealized ancients and even the gods off their pedestals and dresses them in mundane satiric garb. The last part of the passage parodies the tradition of reporting spectacular portents to religious officials for interpretation, and then recording them in Rome's official annals; similar accounts of portents are also featured in epic narratives.

38   **hoc ... more** refers to the virtuous life, the theme of the previous lines

       indigenae "earth-born," a substantive here. Various legends held that early humans were born from trees or mud (cf. **Juvenal 14.35** and 6.12–13, and Vergil *Aeneid* 8.314–15).

vivebant the implied subject is *homines*

39 **diademate** abl. sing.

40 **Saturnus** Saturn was said to have reigned in a golden age of peace and fertility. Ovid *Metamorphoses* 1.89–115 describes life in this age and the transition to a harder existence for humans upon Jupiter's ousting of Saturn (cf. **Persius 5.50**).

40–45 **cum virguncula ... taberna** supply an impf. form of *sum* with each item in this list of noms. (except in 43–44, where *stabat* is more appropriate)

41 **Idaeis ... antris** Jupiter was said to have been born and nursed on Mt. Ida in Asia Minor (although some ancient sources identify this place as the mountain of the same name in Crete)

42 **convivia caelicolarum** a heavy and grand phrase, but also playfully alliterative. The image recalls Homer *Iliad* 1.597–604, where the gods are depicted amusing themselves at a banquet.

43 **puer Iliacus** Ganymede, the beautiful boy from Troy (also called Ilium) whom Jupiter snatched up to be his lover and cupbearer

formonsa ... Herculis uxor Hebe, the goddess of youth, given in marriage to Hercules when he became immortal; she is the handsome Ganymede's female counterpart at the gods' table

44 **ad cyathos** "at the ladle," i.e., serving wine from the mixing-bowl

et a substitution for *nec* here; cf. *nec ... nec ... nec ... aut* in line 50

iam goes with the abl. absolute; Vulcan has an after-work drink, then cleans up

45 **Liparaea ... taberna** abl. of cause (scan the line to see that both endings are long); it explains *nigra*. Lipare is a volcanic island near Sicily (see map); Vergil locates Vulcan's workshop there in a passage that describes the grueling work of the forge (*Aeneid* 8.417). *taberna* has a touch of modernity and humility (it is the word for a craftsman's stall).

46   **prandebat** a mundane term, contrasting with the god's diet of nectar and ambrosia

       sibi dat. of interest, implying they ate casually and alone

46-47   **turba . . . talis** supply *erat*. The gods were once not so numerous, as Hesiod's *Theogony* and other sources indicate. This is probably also a jab at the relatively modern practice of officially deifying emperors.

47-48   **contenta . . . numinibus** the stars stand roughly for "heaven," the gods' residence

48   **Atlanta** acc. sing. Atlas, a Titan, had to hold up the heavens on his shoulders

49   **sortitus** supply *erat*. Jupiter, Pluto, and Neptune drew lots and were assigned the realms of sky, underworld, and ocean, respectively (see Homer *Iliad* 15.187–94).

50   **Sicula . . . coniuge** in Roman accounts (e.g., Ovid *Metamorphoses* 5.385–408), Pluto snatched Persephone in Sicily

       torvos an archaic nom. sing. m. ending, sometimes seen in post-archaic epic; this lends more (mock-)solemnity to the passage

51-52   **nec rota . . . poena** Juvenal moves from the heavens to the underworld for further evidence of this lost age's innocence. In Greek and Roman myth, punishments of notorious criminals took place in the underworld. Juvenal names the punishments but not the criminals. Ixion, who assaulted Juno, was strapped to a rotating wheel; Sisyphus, who tricked the gods, was cursed with his futile uphill boulder-rolling; and Tityus, who tried to rape Jupiter's consort Leto, had his liver repeatedly eaten by vultures. The Furies harassed murderers, especially those who killed family members.

52   **hilares** refers to the absence of criminals undergoing punishment, but perhaps also to a lost era when even the general population of shades was happy (contrast, e.g., the gloomy afterlife of Homer's heroes in *Odyssey* book 11)

       regibus i.e., *rege et regina*

53   **inprobitas . . . aevo** now Juvenal moves from the shades in the underworld to living people and their community values

      admirabilis note the root *miror*; better translated "strange" or "worthy of amazement" than as the misleading English cognate (cf. *prodigiosa*, 62)

54   **credebant** the implied subject is *homines*; in the predicate, supply *esse*. Juvenal now concentrates on early human communities.

      quo the antecedent is *illo aevo*

      morte abl. of means, completing the sense of the gerundive

55   **vetulo** a substantive. The diminutive might imply infirmity, but it also carries a mocking tone that undercuts the reverent description of the old ways.

56   **barbato . . . puer** supply *adsurrexerat*. In Juvenal's day, older men went clean-shaven, but the poet is thinking of the conventional image of rugged old-time Romans.

      licet . . . videret *licet* + subjunctive often indicates a concession; hence, "even if he saw"; i.e., "even if his family owned"

      ipse refers to the younger person in the two examples given

57   **fraga et . . . glandis acervos** the measure of wealth in this comically primitive world. *glandis* is collective sing. and gen. of material. The acorn diet is a commonplace in ancient writing about primitive humans; Juvenal claims they "belched acorns" (6.10).

58   **praecedere** the subject of *erat*, modified by the n. sing. predicate adj.

      quattuor indeclinable; modifies *annis* (an abl. of degree of difference)

59   **adeo** modifies *par*; the phrase parallels *tam venerabile* in 58

60   **nunc** the depraved present. Juvenal represents it much as he does the past, i.e., both critically and comically.

61   **cum tota aerugine** "rust and all," i.e., untouched

<dl>
<dt>62</dt>
<dd>prodigiosa predicate adj; supply est or videtur

fides i.e., the "trustworthiness" reflected in the gesture

Tuscis . . . libellis the Etruscan sacred books (from Etruria; see map) used by Roman religious officials to interpret portents. Strange events such as those listed in 64–70 were generally interpreted as signs of divine anger, and so warranted interpretation and corrective action such as sacrifices.</dd>

<dt>63</dt>
<dd>quaeque the rel. pron. (antecedent fides) plus -que

coronata priests put garlands on animals about to be sacrificed</dd>

<dt>64</dt>
<dd>sanctum "who abides by his oaths"</dd>

<dt>64-65</dt>
<dd>bimembri . . . puero this and the next two dats. are governed by comparo, which takes acc. + dat. bimembris is sometimes applied to Centaurs, and there as probably here it means "half-human, half-animal"</dd>

<dt>65</dt>
<dd>miranti a transferred epithet with comic effect: the plow feels the farmer's amazement. The text of this line is disputed; as printed here, it must contain a hiatus between puero and et.</dd>

<dt>67</dt>
<dd>sollicitus modifying the satirist; can be expanded to "and I'd be anxious"</dd>

<dt>67-69</dt>
<dd>tamquam . . . tamquam asyndeton; vel would be the appropriate conjunction</dd>

<dt>68</dt>
<dd>apium gen. of material. Swarming bees were interpreted as portents—sometimes good, sometimes bad (see, e.g., Vergil Georgics 4.554–58).</dd>

<dt>68-69</dt>
<dd>longa . . . uva culmine delubri the first abl. expresses manner (it may be translated with "in" or "in the shape of"; see Allen & Greenough's New Latin Grammar, section 412N). The second expresses place.</dd>

<dt>70</dt>
<dd>lactis vertice torrens best translated in reverse order. vertice is an abl. of means and lactis is gen. of material (and the key word in the image).</dd>
</dl>

∾ *Parents who teach vice,* Juvenal *Satire* 14.1–55

This enormous poem (Juvenal's second longest) catalogues the vices that parents pass on to their impressionable children, thus warning parents of the consequences of their own moral laxity. The opening passage covers several examples of "inherited" vice (greed, gluttony, cruelty, adultery) and provides illustrations; along the way, Juvenal produces several forceful aphorisms about the malleability of children. This is a good example of the emotional and stylistic range of Juvenal's later satires, where philosophical solemnity alternates with scathing attacks and amusing narrative scenes. The satirist is treating a theme that was common in moral philosophical writing of his day and earlier. Fathers and sons are the focus of much traditional Roman teaching (for example, the famous Republican censor Cato "the Elder" was famous for overseeing his son's education himself and expressing great concern over what kind of behavior his son witnessed; see Plutarch, *Life of Cato* 20). Juvenal expresses the kind of principles Cato espoused, although he is of course not confined to a strictly moral agenda. With this last passage, the student is encouraged to think about this poem's connections to previous works of satire, including the theme of the father-son relationship and its role in moral development. Horace linked his father's teachings to his satiric theory, and Persius paid tribute to his tutor Cornutus with memories and a display of his acquired wisdom. Juvenal, never one to explicitly introduce his personal history into his satire, instead develops the basic idea of the parent-child dynamic into the backdrop of yet another survey of contemporary vice.

1   **sunt** "there are"

Fuscine unknown; the name (from *fuscus*, "dark," "dim") may be punningly linked to the images of shine and staining in line 2

sinistra i.e., harmful. In some manuscripts, a difficult and suspect line follows this one (*et quod maiorum vitia sequiturque minores*).

2   **maculam haesuram** the image works well metaphorically, but there is probably also an allusion to the literal mark made in the censor's rolls (see note on line 50 below) next to names of disgraced citizens

     rebus here the person's or family's name or position. The adj. *nitidis* works well in the "marking" metaphor.

3   **parentes** the subject, deferred until the end of the line, is a shocker

4   **alea** as in **1.88**, an element in society's moral downfall

     et "also," "too"

5   **bullatus** postponed for greater shock value: "even while he still wears the *bulla*" (cf. the note on **Persius 5.31**)

     eadem . . . arma cf. the martial metaphor for gambling at **1.91–92**. The father in this vignette is helping to ensure that the next generation will provide plenty more satiric material.

6   **sperare** along with the dat. *cuiquam . . . propinquo*, governed by *concedet* in 7. *sperare* then looks to *melius de se*; remember that *se* will refer to the sentence's subject.

7   **iuvenis** perhaps refers to the same *heres* in 4; if so, may be translated "as a young man." Alternatively, Juvenal is considering a different individual as he turns to a new vice (and a traditional satiric theme; cf. the gourmands in **Persius 2** and **Juvenal 1**).

7–9 **radere . . . condire . . . mergere** all governed by *didicit* (9)

8   **eodem iure** "in their own sauce," an abl. of place after the pple.

9   **mergere** either "steep" or, as some think, "gulp down" (an unusual sense)

     ficedulas the "fig-pecker" (Ital. *beccafico*; note the root *ficus*) or garden warbler (a European bird that eats both insects and fruits). The rich Trimalchio serves this delicacy at Petronius *Satyricon* 33.

9–10 **nebulone parente et cana . . . gula** hendiadys (cf. **3.211**); in this phrasing, the pple. goes with both nouns to make abl. absolutes. *gula* stands for "gluttony" here as at **1.140**.

10-11   **annus transierit puerum** the reverse of the English phrasing. *transierit* is fut. pf.

11   **nondum** modifies the pple.

12   **barbatos ... magistros** "philosophers," stereotypically bearded
        licet admoveas cf. **13.56–57**; as there, "but" may be supplied
        with the main clause

12-13   **inde ... hinc** i.e., on all sides

13   **lauto ... paratu** *ceno* usually takes an acc. object, but here
        takes an abl. of means (like *vescor*, another eating verb)

14   **magna** not just "large" but "lavish"

        degenerare note the primary sense of the verb (from the root
        genus), and the surprising ending of the line in *culina* rather
        than something more grand or abstract. Juvenal is sarcastically
        describing luxurious dining as an ancestral virtue that the son
        perpetuates (while *real* virtues die out; cf. **Juvenal 8** and **13**).

15   **modicis erroribus** the sort to which Horace confesses at
        1.4.131–32. The phrase is dat., following *aequos*.

16-18   **praecipit ... putat ... docet** the subject is Rutilus (unknown)
        in 18

16   **nostra** that is, of "us" freeborn people

17   **materia ... paribusque elementis** abl. of material without a
        prep., as often in poetry; cf. line 35. *paribus* applies to both
        nouns.

19   **plagarum strepitu** the sound of flogging

19-20   **Sirena ... Antiphates ... Polyphemus** all monsters in Homer's
        Odyssey. The singing Sirens lure men onto an island and to their
        deaths (*Sirena* is acc. sing). Antiphates is king of the man-eating
        Laestrygonians; Juvenal is likening the cruel Rutilus to this char-
        acter ("an Antiphates to his trembling household [*laris*]") and to
        Polyphemus, the gigantic Cyclops who also eats men.

21   **tunc** looks ahead to the *quotiens* clause

        aliquis specifically the slave who was responsible for the
        lintea in 22

22   **lintea** modified by *duo*. These may be napkins (cf. the stolen napkins in Catullus 12) or towels lost at the public baths. The line is strikingly arranged, with the description of the brutal punishment enclosing the small pretext for it.

23   **quid suadet iuveni** "to what course (or mindset) does he persuade the young man?"

23-24   **laetus . . . quem** again referring to Rutilus or his type

24   **inscripta** here meaning marks made by a hot brand

25   **rusticus expectas** "are you so naive as to expect . . ." Although his persona has changed since the "angry" poems, Juvenal still occasionally employs aggressive, accusatory rhetorical questions (see note on **1.63**). A substantive clause follows; *sit* looks to the future. This is Juvenal's only mother-daughter example.

      Largae a name that is attested elsewhere; Juvenal may have chosen it here to suggest the woman's sexual generosity

26   **moechos** i.e., *nomina moechorum*

27   **contexere** construe as "make a list" (of *moechi*)

28   **ter deciens** "thirteen times," also seen spelled *ter decies* or as one word. The number here simply stands for "many" (cf. *duo* at Persius 1.2).

29   **virgo** with the same function as *parvula* at **6.89**; *nunc* in 29 means "as a married woman"

      hac the *mater*, now explicitly guiding her daughter

      pusillas the diminutive sarcastically suggests that the young bride's love-letters (*ceras*) are almost cute

29-30   **fuit . . . implet** asyndeton

30   **ferre** expressing purpose after *dat*; *ceras* is the implied object of both these verbs

      cinaedis in the so-called "O" fragment found in one manuscript of *Satire* 6, Juvenal asserts that homosexual men are the confidants and accomplices of choice for adulterous wives

31-33   **sic natura . . . auctoribus** one of the satirist's more forceful evaluations of human nature

31   **uelocius et citius** pleonasm (GL 692)

32-33 **magnis . . . auctoribus** an abl. absolute, but the smoothest translation is "on high authority." *auctores* function as living exempla; cf. the *auctor* cited at **Horace 1.4.122.**

33   **cum subeant** causal clause

33-34 **unus et alter . . . iuvenes** "one or two youths." Note the attachment of sing. adjs. to a pl. subject and verb.

34   **spernant** potential subjunctive; so is *videas* in line 42

      quibus "in whom" or perhaps "for whom"

35   **Titan** specifically, Prometheus, the Titan who in some accounts created humans out of clay (narrated at Ovid *Metamorphoses* 1.82–88)

36   **ducunt** the subject is *vestigia*

37   **diu** so placed because it modifies *monstrata* rather than the verb

      culpae an appositional gen. with *orbita* (B 202, GL 361)

38   **abstineas . . . damnandis** Juvenal's message to parents, succinctly put. *abstineas* is a substantive here.

      huius i.e., this course of action

38-39 **vel una . . . est** "there is at least one"

39-40 **ne crimina nostra sequantur . . . geniti** the pple. is used substantively. This is the abstract moral motive Juvenal presents for maintaining an upright lifestyle. But later in the poem, the satirist makes an appeal to parents' self-interest too, warning that they may come to harm at the hands of their degenerate children. The worst case is that a son immersed in a life of greed will kill off his father to receive his inheritance sooner (14.210–55).

40   **ex nobis** follows the pple.

40-41 **dociles . . . sumus** the adj. takes a dat. of purpose (on the gerundive, see GL 429 and B 191.3): "easily taught to imitate"

41-43 **Catilinam . . . Brutus . . . Bruti . . . avunculus** the names all stand for types; "a" may be supplied before each name in translation. Catilina (Catiline) led an unsuccessful conspiracy to seize power in the Republic. Brutus is the name of the Republican hero who expelled the kings, but it becomes clear that Juvenal is referring to the assassin of Julius Caesar who bore the same name (and who was a hero to some writers of the early Imperial period). His uncle was Cato of Utica, a Stoic famous for his rigid principles.

45-46 **procul . . . puellae lenonum et . . . parasiti** the command *procul* (supply *ite*) is a conventional warning to the profane or uninitiated to stay away from rites or secrets (e.g., the Sibyl at Vergil *Aeneid* 6.258), but Juvenal adapts the formula to warn low-lifes away from the home. On *parasiti*, see note on **1.139.**

47 **reverentia** certainly a Roman child should show this for his parents, but ancient writers on education also advised parents to mirror this feeling (the same is true of *pietas*)

48 **contempseris** with the same sense as at **6.90.** A bad parent might think that his son's youth (*annos*) makes him immune to influence.

49 **filius infans** even younger than a *puer*

50 **censoris** the censors were magistrates who, among other duties, oversaw public morality and could subject criminal or immoral citizens to a public rebuke or penalty

51-52 **se . . . dederit** "has turned out to be" (+ *similem*)

corpore . . . vultu abls. of specification

52-53 **qui . . . peccet** rel. clause of characteristic; *omnia* is acc. of inner object after *peccet*

54 **nimirum** ironic

55 **haec** the reprimands

tabulas mutare i.e., strike your son from your will. The father will start with reprimands, but he will not be above cold and practical revenge as well. To disinherit a family member was considered shocking, but the possibility was there, just as wheedling *captatores* like those in **Horace 2.5** might find their way into a will.

Illustration Credits

Fig. 1. Portion of William R. Shepherd's plan of Imperial Rome. From William R. Shepherd, *Historical Atlas*. 7th edition, revised. New York: Henry Holt and Co., 1929.

Fig. 2. Map: Locations in Roman Italy mentioned in the texts and notes. Mapping Specialists, Ltd. © 2010, Bolchazy-Carducci Publishers, Inc.

Fig. 3. Graffito of victorious gladiator carrying palm branch (Pompeii, Imperial period). From Jules Fleury [Champfleury, pseud.], *Histoire de la Caricature Antique*. Edited by E. Dentu. Paris: Libraire de la Sociètè des gens de lettres, n.d.

Fig. 4. Terracotta figurines of two comic actors playing a male slave and a *paterfamilias* (Etruria, Republican period). The British Museum. Photograph by and courtesy of Barbara McManus, used with permission.

Fig. 5. Terracotta group of two women conversing (Asia Minor, Hellenistic period). The British Museum. Image available © The Trustees of the British Museum. This photograph by and courtesy of Ann Raia Colaneri, used with permission.

Vocabulary

ā *or* **ab,** *prep.* + *abl.*, from, out of, away from; by (*agent*)

abacus, -ī, *m.*, board, tablet (*for counting*); table

absēns, *gen.* **-entis,** *adj.*, absent

absterreō, -ēre, -uī, -itum, to scare away from, discourage from

abstineō, -ēre, -tinuī, -tentum, to hold away from, abstain from

āc. *See* **atque**

accēdō, -ere, -cēssī, -cēssum, to come to, be added; agree with, assent

accipiō, -ere, -cēpī, -ceptum, to accept, take to oneself, receive

Accius, -ī, *m.*, Accius, an actor

accommodō (1), to fit, apply to

accurrō, -ere, -currī, -cursum, to run, hasten to

ācer, ācris, ācre, *adj.*, sharp; violent, spirited, fierce

acerbus, -a, -um, *adj.*, bitter, harsh

acerra, -ae, *f.*, box for incense

acervus, -ī, *m.*, heap, pile

aconītum, -ī, *n.*, wolfs-bane (*a poisonous plant*)

ad, *prep.* + *acc.*, to, towards

addō, -ere, addidī, additum, to add

addubitō (1), to doubt, question

adeō, *adv.*, so far, thus far, to such a degree

adficiō, -ere, -fēcī, -fectum, to stir (the emotions of), excite

adflō (1), to breathe on, inspire

adhūc, *adv.*, to this point, still

admīrābilis, -e, *adj.*, astonishing, surprising

admittō, -ere, -mīsī, -missum, to admit, allow to come (in)

admoveō, -ēre, -mōvī, -mōtum, to bring to, move near

adnō (1), to swim towards

adnuō, -ere, -nuī, -nūtum, to nod assent to, grant

adrēpō, -ere, -rēpsī, —, to creep towards, steal upon

adsūrgō, -ere, -surrēxī, -surrēctum, to rise up, stand up

adulter, adultrī, *m.*, adulterer

adultera, -ae, *f.*, adultress

aedēs, -ium, *f.pl.*, house

aedīlis, -is, *m.*, aedile (*magistrate in Rome or other Italian town*)

aeger, -gra, -grum, *adj.*, ill, ailing

Aelia, -ae, *f.,* Aelia, a woman's name

aēnus, -a, -um, *adj.,* of bronze

aequālis, -e, *adj.,* equal, even

aequor, -oris, *n.,* level surface; surface of the sea

aequus, -a, -um, *adj.,* even, fair

āēr, āēris, *m.,* air, sky

aerūgō, -inis, *f.,* copper-rust, verdigris

aerumna, -ae, *f.,* hardship, affliction

Aesernīnus, -a, -um, *adj.,* from Aesernia, a town in Samnium

aetās, -ātis, *f.,* life-time, age

aevum, -ī, *n.,* time period, age

Agamemnonidēs, -ae, *m.,* son of Agamemnon; i.e., Orestes (*mythical hero*)

ager, agrī, *m.,* land, field; estate

agitō (1), to put in motion, shake; deliberate about

agna, -ae, *f.,* ewe lamb

agō, -ere, ēgī, āctum, to do; drive, urge, push; act a part; (*in imperative*) come, come now

agrestis, -e, *adj.,* rustic, of the country

āiō, ais, ait, *impf.* **āiēbam,** *defective verb,* to say, assert

alapa, -ae, *f.,* box on the ear; slapstick

albātus, -a, -um, *adj.,* clothed in white

Albīnus, -ī, *m.,* Albinus, an addressee of Lucilius

albus, -a, -um, *adj.,* white, bright

Albius, -ī, *m.,* Albus, a man's name

ālea, -ae, *f.,* dice; gambling; venture

algeō, -ēre, ālsī, —, to be cold, shiver

aliēnus, -a, -um, *adj.,* belonging to another

aliquis, aliqua, aliquid, *indef. pron.,* somebody, something

alius, -a, -ud, *adj.,* other

alō, -ere, aluī, altum/alitum, to nourish, rear

Alpēs, -ium, *f.,* the Alps, the mountains just north of Italy

alter, -tera, -terum, *adj. and pron.,* another; one or other of two

altercor, -ārī, -ātus sum, to dispute, argue

amāns, -antis, *m./f.,* lover

ambiguus, -a, -um, *adj.,* doubtful, of two possible kinds

ambō, -ae, ambō, *adj.,* both, the two

Ambrosius, -ī, *m.,* Ambrosius, a flute-player

amictus, -ūs, *m.,* cloak, mantle

amīcus, -ī, *m.,* friend, client

āmittō, -ere, -mīsī, -missum, to let go, lose

amnis, -is, *m.,* stream, river

amō (1), to love

amor, -ōris, *m.,* love, passion

amplexus, -ūs, *m.,* embrace

amplius, *adv.,* more

an, *conj.,* whether; or; or perhaps

anceps, *gen.* **-cipitis,** *adj.,* uncertain, undecided

anguis, -is, *m./f.,* snake, serpent

angustus, -a, -um, *adj.,* narrow

anima, -ae, *f.,* breath, life

animal, -ālis, *n.,* animal, living being

animus, -ī, *m.,* soul, spirit, mind, heart; (*in pl.*) anger, passion

annus, -ī, *m.,* year

ante, *adv.,* previously, first; *prep.* + *acc.,* before, in front of

antīcus. *See* **antīquus**

Antigonē, -ēs, *f.,* Antigone, a tragic heroine

Antiphatēs, -ae, *m.,* Antiphates, a mythical cannibalistic king

antīquus, -a, -um, *adj.,* former, ancient

antrum, -ī, *n.,* cave

ānulus, -ī, *m.,* ring, signet-ring

aper, aprī, *m.,* wild boar

apertus, -a, -um, *adj.,* open, uncovered, candid

apis, -is, *f.,* bee

apium, -ī, *n.,* celery, parsley

appōnō, -ere, -posuī, -positum, to apply to; reckon (*in accounting*)

aptus, -a, -um, *adj.,* accomodating to

apud, *prep.* + *acc.,* at, beside, near, by, before

Āpula, -ae, *f.,* Apula, a woman's name

aqua, -ae, *f.,* water

arātrum, -ī, *n.,* plough

arca, -ae, *f.,* cupboard; chest, coffer

arcānus, -a, -um, *adj.,* secret, private

arcessō, -ere, -īvī, -ītum, to send for, summon

ārdeō, -ēre, ārsī, ārsum, to burn, be ablaze

ārea, -ae, *f.,* threshing-floor

argentum, -ī, *n.,* silver

arma, -ōrum, *n.pl.,* armor, weapons, equipment

armiger, -erī, *m.,* armor-bearer, squire

arō (1), to plough

Arrētium, -ī, *n.,* Arretium, a town in Etruria

ars, artis, *f.,* method, craft, skill

artifex, *gen.* **-icis,** *adj.,* of a craftsman, skilfully made

arx, arcis, *f.,* fortress; hilltop, retreat

as, assis, *m.,* penny

ascendō, -ere, ascendī, ascēnsum, to climb up, ascend

Āsiānus, -a, -um, *adj.,* of Asia

asinus, -ī, *m.,* donkey, ass

aspiciō, -ere, -spexī, -spectum, to look at, behold

ast. *See* **at**

astrum, -ī, *n.,* star

Asturicus, -ī, *m.,* Asturicus, a man's name

astūtus, -a, -um, *adj.,* clever, sly, cunning

at *or* **ast,** *conj.,* but, moreover, on the other hand

Ātellānus, -a, -um, *adj.*, of an Atellan farce (*comic play of Campania*)

āter, -tra, -trum, *adj.*, black, dark; malevolent

Athēnae, -ārum, *f.*, Athens, the most famous city in Greece

Atlās, -antis, *m.*, Atlas, a Titan who was forced to hold up the earth

atque *or* **ac,** *conj.*, and, and even; (*in comparisons*) than

attendō, -ere, -tendī, -tentum, to attend to, direct attention to

auctor, -ōris, *m./f.*, authority; model, example

auctōrō (1), to hire oneself out

audāx, *gen.* **-ācis,** *adj.*, daring, bold

audeō, -ēre, ausus sum, —, to dare, venture

audiō, -īre, -īvī, -ītum, to hear, listen to

auferō, -ferre, abstulī, ablātum, to take away; cease from, stop + *inf.*

Aufidus, -ī, *m.*, the Aufidus, a river of Apulia

aulaeum, -ī, *n.*, hanging, curtain

auricula, -ae, *f.*, ear, little ear (*dimin.*)

auris, -is, *f.*, ear

aurum, -ī, *n.*, gold

aut, *conj.*, or; **aut . . . aut,** either . . . or

autem, *conj.*, moreover, but, and, now

Autonoē, -ēs, *f.*, Autonoe, aunt of the god Dionysus in myth

auxilium, -ī, *n.*, help, aid

avāritia, -ae, *f.*, greed, avarice

avārus, -a, -um, *adj.*, greedy, grasping

āvellō, -ere, -vellī *or* **-vulsī, -vulsum,** to pull away, tear away

avia, -ae, *f.*, grandmother

avidus, -a, -um, *adj.*, over-eating

avunculus, -ī, *m.*, maternal uncle

axis, -is, *m.*, sky

Baius, -ī, *m.*, Baius, a man's name

balneum, -ī, *n.*, bath

barba, -ae, *f.*, beard

barbātus, -a, -um, *adj.*, bearded

Bathyllus, -ī, *m.*, Bathyllus, a dancer in pantomimes

beātus, -a, -um, *adj.*, prosperous, blessed

bellus, -a, -um, *adj.*, pretty, fine, agreeable

bēlua, -ae, *f.*, beast, animal

bene, *adv.*, well, aptly, properly

benīgnus, -a, -um, *adj.*, favorable, beneficent

bidēns, -entis, *m.*, two-pronged pick, hoe

bīlis, -is, *f.*, gall, bile

bimembris, -e, *adj.*, having limbs of two kinds, having qualities of two species

bis, *adv.*, twice, two times

blanditia, -ae, *f.*, flattery, wheedling

blandus, -a, -um, *adj.*, coaxing, seductive

blaterō (1), to babble, prate

bōlētus, -ī, *m.*, mushroom

bonus, -a, -um, *adj.*, good

bōs, bovis, *m./f.*, ox, cow

bracchium, -ī, *n.*, forearm, arm

brevis, -e, *adj.*, small, narrow, shallow

Brūtus, -ī, *m.*, M. Iunius Brutus, one of the assassins of Julius Caesar

bulla, -ae, *f.*, knob; child's amulet

bullātus, -a, -um, *adj.*, wearing the *bulla*

cachinnō (1), to laugh immoderately, cackle

cadō, -ere, cecidī, cāsum, to fall, collapse

caedō, -ere, cecīdī, caesum, to kill, slaughter

caelebs, *gen.* -libis, *adj.*, unmarried, single

caelicola, -ae, *m./f.*, one who dwells in heaven, god

caenum, -ī, *n.*, dirt, filth, mud, mire

calcō (1), to tread on

Calēnum, -ī, *n.*, Calenum, fine wine from the city of Cales in Campania

caleō, -ēre, -uī, —, grow warm, grow hot

callidus, -a, -um, *adj.*, expert, crafty

Callirhoē, -ēs, *f.*, Callirhoe, a female character in a mime or love story; the title of said work

Camēna, -ae, *f.*, Camena, a Roman deity equated with the Greek Muses

campus, -ī, *m.*, field

candidus, -a, -um, *adj.*, dazzling white; splendid-looking

Canīcula, -ae, *f.*, Canicula, the Dog-star (Sirius)

canīnus, -a, -um, *adj.*, of a dog, canine

cānitiēs, ēī, f., gray hair, old age

Canōpus, -ī, *m.*, Canopus, a town in Egypt

cantharus, -ī, *m.*, tankard, large-bellied drinking vessel

cantō (1), to sing

cantus, -ūs, *m.*, singing, song

cānus, -a, -um, *adj.*, white, hoary, gray

capax, *gen.* -ācis, *adj.*, spacious, able to hold much

caper, -prī, *m.*, goat

capiō, -ere, cēpī, captum, to capture, seize, hold

captō (1), to snatch at eagerly or frequently, try for

caput, -itis, *n.*, head

carcer, -eris, *m.*, jail

carmen, -inis, *n.*, song, poetic work

cassus, -a, -um, *adj.*, empty, shelled

castīgō (1), to chastise, censure

cāsus, -ūs, *m.*, event, chance occurrence; risk, hazard; misfortune

catēna, -ae, *f.*, chain, fetter

cathedra, -ae, *f.*, arm chair; sedan-chair

Catilīna, -ae, *m.,* L. Sergius Catilina (Catiline), Republican politician and leader of a failed conspiracy

Catullus, -ī, *m.,* Catullus, a writer of mimes in the Imperial period

cauda, -ae, *f.,* tail; penis

causa, -ae, *f.,* cause, reason, motive; legal case

cautē, *adv.,* warily, cautiously

cautus, -a, -um, *adj.,* wary, careful

caveō, -ēre, cāvī, cautum, to beware, take heed

cēdō, -ere, cēssī, cēssum, to withdraw, go away

celsus, -a, -um, *adj.,* lofty, high

cēna, -ae, *f.,* dinner

cēnō (1), to dine, take a meal

cēnsor, -ōris, *m.,* censor, moral judge

centēnī, -ae, -a, *adj.,* group of one hundred

centum, *adj.,* one hundred

cēra, -ae, *f.,* wax; writing-tablet

cernō, -ere, crēvī, crētum, to distinguish, discern

certē, *adv.,* surely, undoubtedly

certō (1), to contend, compete, dispute

certus, -a, -um, *adj.,* settled, definite

cervīx, -īcis, *f.,* neck

cēssō (1), to rest, be inactive

cētarīum, -ī, *n.,* fish-pond

charta, -ae, *f.,* paper

Chīrōn, -ōnis, *m.,* Chiron, a centaur

chīronomos, -ī, *m.,* gesticulator, performer of pantomime

choraulēs, -ae, *m.,* flute-player

Chrȳsogonus, -ī, *m.,* Chrysogonus, a singer

cibus, -ī, *m.,* food

cinaedus, -ī, *m.,* sodomite, effeminate man

circēnsēs, -ium, *m.pl.,* games in the circus, races

circum, *prep.* + *acc.,* around, about

cista, -ae, *f.,* chest, box

cithara, -ae, *f.,* cithara, lute

citharoedus, -ī, *m.,* player of the cithara

citius, *compar. adv.,* more quickly

cito, *adv.,* quickly, speedily, soon

cīvis, -is, *m./f.,* citizen; fellow-citizen

clam, *adv.,* secretly, privately

clāmō (1), to cry out, proclaim

clāmor, -ōris, *m.,* shout, noise

clāmōsus, -a, -um, *adj.,* full of noise and clamor

clārē, *adv.,* aloud, clearly

clārus, -a, -um, *adj.,* clear, bright

claudō, -ere, clausī, clausum *or* **clūdō, -ere, clūsī, clūsum,** to close, shut

clūdō. *See* **claudō**

clūnis, -is, *m./f.,* buttock, haunch

Cluviēnus, -ī, *m.,* Cluvienus, a man's name

cognitor, -ōris, *m.,* advocate, attorney

cōgō, -ere, coēgī, coāctum, to
force, compel
collēga, -ae, *m.*, colleague,
associate
colō, -ere, coluī, cultum, to live
in, inhabit
colossus, -ī, *m.*, gigantic statue,
colossus
columba, -ae, *f.*, dove, pigeon
comedō, -ēsse, -ēdī, -ēsum *or*
-ēstum, to eat up, squander
comes, -itis, *m./f.*, companion,
comrade
comitō (1) *or* **comitor, -ārī,**
-ātus sum, to accompany,
follow, attend
comminuō, -ere, -uī, -ūtum, to
break up, lessen
committō, -ere, -mīsī, -missum,
to commit, entrust
commodus, -a, -um, *adj.*,
advantageous, suitable
cōmoedus, -ī, *m.*, comedic actor
comparō (1), to match, compare
(*acc.*) to (*dat.*)
compīlō (1), to rob
compitum, -ī, *n.*, cross-roads
comprimō, -ere, -pressī,
-pressum, to press together,
close
concēdō, -ere, -cēssī, -cēssum,
to give up, allow; concede,
give way to + *dat.*; go over
to, merge with + *in* and *acc.*
concors, *gen.* **concordis,** *adj.*,
agreeing, harmonious,
united
condiō, -īre, -īvī *or* **-iī, -itum,**
to preserve, season

condō, -ere, -didī, -ditum, to
bury
condūcō, -ere, -dūxī, -ductum,
to rent
cōnferō, -ferre, -tulī, -lātum, to
bring together, contribute
congerō, -ere, -gessī, -gestum,
to pile together, collect
coniugium, -ī, *n.*, marriage; (by
metonymy) spouse
coniūnx, -iugis, *m./f.*, spouse
cōnōpeum, -ī, *n.*, mosquito net;
bed fitted with a net
conparō. *See* **comparō**
conpōnō, -ere, -posuī, -positum,
to match, put together
cōnscendō, -ere, -scendī,
-scēnsum, to climb up,
board a ship
cōnscia, -ae, *f.*, female
accomplice, confidant
cōnsentiō, -īre, -sēnsī, -sēnsum,
to agree, be of accord
cōnsīdō, -ere, -sēdī, -sessum,
to sit down, settle
cōnsilium, -ī, *n.*, deliberation,
advice
cōnspuō, -ere, —, ūtum, to spit,
spew
cōnstāns, *gen.* **-antis,** *adj.*, firm,
steady
cōnstō, -stāre, -stitī, -stātum,
to be composed of, consist of
cōnstruō, -ere, -strūxī,
-structum, to heap up
together, pile up
cōnsūmō, -ere, -sūmpsī,
-sūmptum, to consume,
spend

contemnō, -ere, -tēmpsī, -temptum, to think nothing of, belittle, slight

contemplor, -ārī, -ātus sum, to survey, gaze upon

contentus, -a, -um, *adj.,* contented or satisfied with + *abl.*

contexō, -ere, -texuī, -textum, to weave together

contrā, *adv.,* in turn, on the other hand

contrahō, -ere, -trāxī, -tractum, draw in, draw down

convīva, -ae, *m.,* table-companion, guest

convīvium, -ī, *n.,* banquet, social meal

convomō, -ere, —, —, to vomit on

cōpia, -ae, *f.,* supply, stock

cor, cordis, *n.,* heart, mind, spirit

Cordus, -ī, *m.,* Cordus, a man's name

Corinthus, -ī, *m.,* Corinthus, an actor

Cornūtus, -ī, *m.,* Cornutus, the Stoic tutor of Persius

corōna, -ae, *f.,* crown, wreath

corōnō (1), to garland, wreathe

corpus, -oris, *n.,* body

corripiō, -ere, -ripuī, -reptum, to seize; reproach

corrumpō, -ere, -rūpī, -ruptum, to destroy, mar

corruptor, -ōris, *m.,* seducer, adulterer

cortex, -icis, *m./f.,* cork; flotation device made of cork

crassus, -a, -um, *adj.,* thick

Crassus, -ī, *m.,* M. Licinius Crassus, wealthy colleague of Julius Caesar and Pompey

Cratīnus, -ī, *m.,* Cratinus, a comic poet of classical Athens

crēdō, -ere, -didī, -ditum, to have trust in + *dat.*; to believe, think

crepida, -ae, *f.,* slipper, sandal

crepō, -āre, -uī, -itum, to rattle, make a sound

crēscō, -ere, crēvī, crētum, to thrive, multiply

crīmen, -inis, *n.,* crime; charge

Crispīnus, -ī, *m.,* Crispinus, a Stoic sermonizer

crūdus, -a, -um, *adj.,* harsh, cruel; raw, undigested

crux, -ucis, *f.,* cross

cubitum, -ī, *n.,* elbow

culīna, -ae, *f.,* kitchen; cuisine

culmen, -inis, *n.,* top, summit

culpa, -ae, *f.,* sin, fault

cultus, -a, -um, *adj.,* cultivated, tilled

cum, *conj.,* when, since; *prep.* + *abl.,* with; **-cum,** *enclitic prep. affixed to abl.,* with

cumera, -ae, *f.,* grain-bin

cumulus, -ī, *m.,* heap, pile

cūnae, -ārum, *f.pl.,* cradle

cūnctus, -a, -um, *adj.,* all together, the whole, entire

cuneus, -ī, *m.,* wedge; wedge-shaped seating area

cupīdō, -inis, *f.,* desire, longing; greed

cupiō, -ere, cupīvī, cupītum, to long for, desire

cūr, *interr. adv.,* why, for what reason

cūra, -ae, *f.,* care, concern; source of concern

cūrō (1), to give attention to, look after

cursus, -ūs, *m.,* course, flow, onrush

custōs, -ōdis, *m./f.,* guardian, watchman

cyathus, -ī, *m.,* ladle; drinking-cup

cynicus, -a, -um, *adj.,* of the Cynic school of philosophy; (*as a noun*) Cynic philosopher

Dāma, -ae, *m.,* Dama, a man's name (*common among slaves*)

Damasippus, -ī, *m.,* Damasippus, a man's name

damnō (1), to condemn

damnōsus, -a, -um, *adj.,* ruinous, detrimental

Dāvus, -ī, *m.,* Davus, slave of Horace

dē, *prep. + abl.,* from, about, concerning

dēbeō, -ēre, -uī, -itum, to owe; be obligated, must

dēcēdō, -ere, -cessī, -cessum, to withdraw; cease

dēcerpō, -ere, -cerpsī, -cerptum, to gather, pluck

deciēns, *adv.,* ten times

dēcipiō, -ere, -cēpī, -ceptum, to mislead, deceive

dēcoctus, -a, -um, *adj.,* boiled down

decōrus, -a, -um, *adj.,* fine-looking; seemly

dēdō, -ere, dēdidī, dēditum, to give, devote

dēfendō, -ere, -fendī, -fēnsum, to defend, support

dēfēnsor, -ōris, *m./f.,* defender, advocate

dēfodiō, -ere, -fōdī, -fōssum, to dig up

dēgenerō (1), to fall short of, disgrace

deinde, *adv.,* then, next, afterwards

dēlectō (1), to attract

dēlūbrum, -ī, *n.,* shrine, sanctuary, temple

dēmittō, -ere, -mīsī, -missum, to insert, thrust

dēns, dentis, *m.,* tooth

dēpōnō, -ere, -posuī, -positum, lay down, entrust, lay aside

dēpōscō, -ere, -popōscī, —, to demand, ask for, require

dēpositum, -ī, *n.,* something entrusted; a deposit

dēprendō, -ere, -endī, -ēnsum, to seize, catch; discover to be

dēsum, -esse, -fuī, -futūrum, to neglect, fail + *dat.*

dēterius, *compar. adv.,* more poorly, worse

dēterreō, -ēre, -uī, -itum, to deter, discourage from

Deucalion, -ōnis, *m.,* Deucalion, a character in myth

deus, -ī, *m.,* god, deity

dexter, -tera, -terum, *adj.,* on the right side, right

dextra, -ae, *f.,* right hand

diadēma, -matis, *n.,* royal headband, crown

dīcō, -ere, dīxī, dictum, to say, tell of, recite

dictō (1), to dictate for writing

dictum, -ī, *n.,* word, saying

dīdūcō, -ere, dūxī, ductum, to divide, separate

diēs, -ēī, *m.,* day

differō, -ferre, distulī, dīlātum, to delay, put off

diffundō, -ere, -fūdī, -fūsum, to pour around, spread

digitus, -ī, *m.,* finger

dignus, -a, -um, *adj.,* deserving, worthy of + *abl.*

dīligō, -ere, -lēxī, -lēctum, to single out; esteem, love

dīmittō, -ere, -mīsī, -missum, to let go, send away

dīnōscō, -ere, —, —, to distinguish, discern

discēdō, -ere, -cēssī, -cēssum, to give way, depart

dīscō, -ere, didicī, —, to learn

discursus, -ūs, *m.,* running to and fro, running about

dispēnsātor, -ōris, *m.,* steward, treasurer

dispōnō, -ere, -posuī, -positum, to distribute, arrange

dissimilis, -e, *adj.,* unlike, dissimilar

dītior, ditius, *adj.,* wealthier

diū, *adv.,* for a long time

dīves, *gen.* **-itis,** *adj.,* rich, wealthy

dīvidō, -ere, -vīsī, -vīsum, to divide, distibute

dīvīnus, -a, -um, *adj.,* divine, immortal

dīvitiae, -ārum, *f.pl.,* riches, wealth

dīvus, -ī, *m.,* god, deity

dō, dare, dedī, datum, to give

doceō, -ēre, docuī, doctum, to teach, show

docilis, -e, *adj.,* easily taught, tractable

doctus, -a, -um., *adj.,* learned, expert

documentum, -ī, *n.,* lesson, example

doleō, -ēre, -uī, -itūrum, to suffer

dolōsē, *adv.,* cunningly, deceitfully

domesticus, -a, -um, *adj.,* domestic, of the home

dominus, -ī, *m.,* master of a household

Domitius, -ī, *m.,* Domitius, an ancestor of Nero

domus, domūs, *f.,* house, home; *locative* **domī,** at home; *acc.* **domum,** toward home

dōnec, *conj.,* until

dōnō (1), to make a gift of, present

dormiō, -īre, -īvī, -ītum, to sleep

drachma, -ae, *f.,* drachma (*Greek coin*)

dubitō (1), to hesitate
dubium, -ī, *n.*, doubt, uncertainty
dūcō, -ere, dūxī, ductum, to lead; take on
dulcis, -e, *adj.*, pleasant, delightful
dum, *conj.*, while, during the time
duo, -ae, -o, *adj.*, two
dūrō (1), strengthen, make firm
dūrus, -a, -um, *adj.*, hard, harsh, brazen

ēbulliō, -īre, —, —, to bubble out
ecce, *interj.*, look! behold! see!
ecferō. *See* **efferō**
Echīōn, -ōnis, *m.*, Echion, a cithara-player
ecquis, ecquid, *interr. pron.*, any one, anything
ēdictum, -ī, *n.*, announcement, edict
ēdō, -ere, -didī, -ditum, to utter, proclaim
efferō, -ferre, extulī, ēlātum, to carry, bring forth
effigiēs, -ēī, *f.*, statue, portrait
effugiō, -ere, -fūgī, —, to flee, escape
effundō, -ere, -fūdī, -fūsum, to pour forth, shower
egeō, -ēre, -uī, —, to need, suffer want of + *gen. or abl.*
ego, *pers. pron.*, I
ēgregius, -a, -um, *adj.*, distinguished, honorable

Electra, -ae, *f.*, Electra, daughter of Agamemnon and sister of Orestes
elementum, -ī, *n.*, elements, principles
ēlevō (1), to lift; make light of, disparage
emāx, *gen.* **-ācis,** *adj.*, fond of buying, haggling
emō, -ere, ēmī, emptum, to buy, purchase
ēnārrābilis, -e, *adj.*, able to be described or related
enim, *conj.*, certainly, for
eō, īre, iī, itum, to go, proceed
eōdem, *adv.*, to the same place; for the same purpose
Eppia, -ae, *f.*, Eppia, a woman's name
epulum, -ī, *n.*, banquet, feast
equester, -tris, -tre, *adj.*, of an equestrian
equidem, *adv.*, indeed, truly, for my part
equus, -ī, *m.*, horse, steed
ergastulum, -ī, *n.*, workhouse; inmates of a workhouse, chain-gang
erilis, -e, *adj.*, of a master or mistress
ēripiō, -ere, -ripuī, -reptum, to snatch, tear away
errō (1), to wander, roam
errō, -ōnis, *m.*, runaway slave
error, -ōris, *m.*, wandering, mistake, delusion
et, *adv.*, and, also; even, actually; and yet; **et . . . et,** both . . . and

etenim, *conj.*, and in fact, for, indeed

etiam, *conj*, also, indeed

euge, *interj.*, well done! good!

Euphrānor, -ōris, *m.*, Euphranor, a famous sculptor of classical Athens

Eupolis, -is *or* **-idis,** *m.*, Eupolis, a comic poet of classical Athens

Euryalus, -ī, *m.*, Euryalus, a gladiator

ēvādō, -ere, -vāsī, -vāsum, to evade, escape

ēvellō, -ere, -vellī, -vulsum, to pull out

ex, *prep.* + *abl.*, out of, from; instead of

exāmen, -inis, *n.*, swarm of bees; pointer of a scale

exanimis, -e, *adj.*, breathless, lifeless

exanimō (1), to kill, take the life from

excerpō, -ere, -cerpsī, -cerptum, to pick out, choose

excipiō, -ere, -cēpī, -ceptum, to receive

excutiō, -ere, -cussī, -cussum, to shake out, search

exemplum, -ī, *n.*, example, model

exhorrēscō, -ere, -horruī, —, to be terrified at, shudder at

exiguus, -a, -um, *adj.*, small, brief

eximō, -ere, -ēmī, -emptum, to remove

exodium, -ī, *n.*, comic afterpiece; comic theatrical interlude

exoptō (1), to long for, wish

expiō (1), to purify, cleanse ritualistically

exprimō, -ere, -pressī, -pressum, to model, give an impression of

expungō, -ere, -pūnxī, -pūnctum, to prick; mark off (*on a list*)

exspectō (1), to expect, anticipate

exspēs, *adj.*, hopeless

exta, -ōrum, *n.pl.*, entrails, organs

extendō, -ere, -tendī, -tentum *or* **-tēnsum,** to stretch out, straighten

extrā, *adv.*, on the outside, without; *prep.* + *acc.*, outside of

Fabiī, -ōrum, *m.pl.*, the Fabii, a noble family

Fabrāteria, -ae, *f.*, Fabrateria, a town in Latium

fābula, -ae, *f.*, tale, story

facilis, -e, *adj.*, easy

faciō, -ere, fēcī, factum, to do, make

fallō, -ere, fefellī, falsum, to fail, disappoint; beguile

falsus, -a, -um, *adj.*, wrong, erroneous; false, lying

falx, falcis, *f.*, sickle, reaping hook

fāma, -ae, *f.*, reputation; infamy

fāmōsus, -a, -um, *adj.,*
celebrated, famed, notorious
farrāgō, -inis, *f.,* cattle-fodder,
mash, hodge-podge
fās, *indecl. noun,* divine law;
what is lawful or right
fateor, -ērī, fassus sum, to
admit, acknowledge
fātum, -ī, *n.,* destiny, will of the
gods
faucēs, -ium, *f.pl.,* throat, jaws
Faunus, -ī, *m.,* Faunus, a rustic
god
fēcundus, -a, -um, *adj.,* fertile
fēlīx, *gen.* **-īcis,** *adj.,* lucky,
happy
fēmina, -ae, *f.,* woman
ferō, ferre, tulī, lātum, to carry,
bring; bear, endure
ferrum, -ī, *n.,* iron, sword
fertum, -ī, *n.,* sacrificial cake
ferveō, -ēre, —, —, to boil,
seethe
fēstus, -a, -um, *adj.,* festive, of
a holiday
fētus, -a, -um, *adj.,* pregnant,
breeding
fētus, -ūs, *m.,* offspring,
progeny
fibra, -ae, *f.,* entrails
fībula, -ae, *f.,* fastener, clasp
fīcedula, -ae, *f.,* fig-pecker
fīctus, -a, -um, *adj.,* false,
fictitious
fidēlis, -e, *adj.,* faithful, loyal
fidēs, -eī, *f.,* faith, honesty
fīgō, -ere, fīxī, fīxum, to fix,
affix
fīlia, -ae, *f.,* daughter

fīlius, -ī, *m.,* son, child
findō, -ere, fidī, fissum, to
cleave, split
fingō, -ere, fīnxī, fīctum, to
imagine, mold, form
fīnis, -is, *m.,* boundary, limit
fīō, fierī, —, —, to come into
being, to become, arise
firmus, -a, -um, *adj.,* strong,
unyielding
Flaccus, -ī, *m.,* Flaccus, a
cognomen (*belonging to both
Horace and Persius*); (*in pl.*)
the Flacci (*a noble family*)
flagellum, -ī, *n.,* whip, lash
flagrō (1), to blaze, burn
flamma, -ae, *f.,* flame, blaze
flūctus, -ūs, *m.,* wave, surge
flūmen, -inis, *n.,* stream,
moving water
fluō, -ere, fluxī, fluxum, to
flow, run down
foedus, -a, -um, *adj.,* filthy,
shocking
foedus, -eris, *n.,* contract, pact
follis, -is, *m.,* purse
fonticulus, -ī, *m.,* little spring,
fountain
fōrma, -ae, *f.,* form, appearance;
beauty, good looks
formīdō (1), to dread, fear
fōrmō (1), to shape, mold
fōrmōnsus, -a, -um, *adj.,*
beautiful, shapely, handsome
fors, fortis, *f.,* chance; (*in abl.*)
perhaps, by chance
forsitan, *adv.,* perhaps
fortassis, *adv.,* perhaps, possibly
fortis, -e, *adj.,* strong, resolute

fortūna, -ae, *f.*, fortune, circumstances

fortūnō (1), to bless, make prosperous or fortunate

forulī, -ōrum, *m.pl.*, book-case

forum, -ī, *n.*, forum, market place

frāga, -ōrum, *n.pl.*, strawberries

frangō, -ere, frēgī, frāctum, to break, shatter

frīgēscō, -ere, —, —, to become cold, be chilly

fritillus, -ī, *m.*, dice-box

frīvolus, -a, -um, *adj.*, paltry, small; (*as a n. pl. noun*) trifles, small possessions

frōns, frontis, *f.*, forehead, face

frūgāliter, *adv.*, frugally

frūmentum, -ī, *n.*, corn, grain

Frusinō, -ōnis, *m.*, Frusino, a town in Latium

frūstrā, *adv.*, to no purpose, in vain

frūstum, -ī, *n.*, piece, bit (*of food*)

fugāx, *gen.* **-ācis,** *adj.*, fleeing, fugitive

fugiō, -ere, fūgī, fugitum, to flee, take flight

fugitīvus, -ī, *m.*, fugitive; runaway slave

fulciō, -īre, fulsī, fultum, to prop up, support

fūmō (1), to smoke

fundō, -ere, fūdī, fūsum, (1), to pour

fundus, -ī, *m.*, bottom

fūnus, -eris, *n.*, funeral; corpse; death

fūr, fūris, *m./f.*, thief

furca, -ae, *f.*, fork, stocks (*instrument of punishment*)

furcifer, -erī, *m.*, gallows-rogue, rascal

Furia, -ae, *f.*, a Fury, an avenging goddess

Fūrius, -ī, *m.*, Furius, a man's name

furō, -ere, —, —, to rage, rave

furor, -ōris, *m.*, madness, delirium

fūrtim, *adv.*, by stealth, clandestinely

Fuscīnus, -ī, *m.*, Fuscinus, a man's name (*addressee of Juvenal*)

Galba, -ae, *m.*, S. Sulpicius Galba, emperor after Nero

banniō, -īre, —, —, to yelp, squeal

gaudeō, -ēre, gāvīsus sum, —, to rejoice; delight in + *abl.*

gaudium, -ī, *n.*, joy, gladness

gelidus, -a, -um, *adj.*, cold, chilly

gelō (1), to make freeze, make congeal with cold

Geminī, -ōrum, *m.pl.*, the Twins, the constellation Gemini (*representing Castor and Pollux*)

gemma, -ae, *f.*, signet ring, gem

gemō, -ere, -uī, -itum, to bemoan, bewail

gener, -erī, *m.*, son-in-law

generōsus, -a, -um, *adj.*, nobly born, well-bred

genū, -ūs, *n.,* knee
genuīnus, -ī, *m.,* jaw-tooth, molar
gestiō, -īre, -īvī, —, to be eager; delight in + *inf.*
gestus, -ūs, *m.,* motion, gesture
gignō, -ere, genuī, genitum, to beget, bear
gladiātor, -ōris, *m.,* gladiator
gladius, -ī, *m. or* **gladium, -ī,** *n.,* sword
glāns, glandis, *f.,* acorn; nut
Glaphyrus, -ī, *m.,* Glaphyrus, a musician
gnātus. *See* **nātus**
gradus, -ūs, *m.,* step, level
Graecus, -a, -um, *adj.,* Greek
Graius, -a, -um, *adj.,* Greek
grānāria, -ōrum, *n.pl.,* granary
grandis, -e, *adj.,* abundant, large, great
gravis, -e, *adj.,* heavy; noxious
grex, gregis, *m.,* flock, herd
gula, -ae, *f.,* gullet; palate; gluttony
gurges, -itis, *m.,* current, whirlpool
Gyara, -ōrum, *n.pl.,* Gyara, a small island in the Aegean sea

habeō, -ēre, -uī, -itum, to hold, have
habitus, -ūs, *m.,* bearing; dress
haereō, -ēre, haesī, haesum, to hang, stick, linger
hāmus, -ī, *m.,* hook, fish-hook
hauriō, -īre, hausī, haustum, to draw off; drink

haustus, -ūs, *m.,* drawing off (*of liquid*)
haut *or* **haud,** *adv.,* not at all, by no means
hēmīna, -ae, *f.,* half a *sextarius*; half-pint measure
hercule, *interj.,* by Hercules!
Hercules, -is, *m.,* Hercules, Greek demigod
hērēs, -ēdis, *m./f.,* an heir, successor
hiātus, -ūs, *m.,* an opening, gap
hībernus, -a, -um, *adj.,* of or in winter, wintry
hīc, haec, hoc *or* **hōc,** *pron.,* this
hīc, *adv.,* in this place, here
hilaris, -e, *adj.,* cheerful, merry
hinc, *adv.,* from this place, hence
Hispulla, -ae, *f.,* Hispulla, a woman's name
hodiē, *adv.,* today, now
holus, -eris, *n.,* vegetables, greens
homō, -inis, *m./f.,* human being, person
honestus, -a, -um, *adj.,* honorable, respected
honor, -ōris, *m.,* honor, esteem; public office
hōra, -ae, *f.,* hour
horreō, -ēre, -uī, —, to shiver
horridus, -a, -um, *adj.,* disheveled, wild
hortor, -ārī, -ātus sum, to exhort, urge strongly
hortulus, -ī, *m.,* little garden
hortus, -ī, *m.,* garden
hospes, -itis, *m.,* guest, visitor

hospitium, -ī, *n.,* lodging,
shelter

hostis, -is, *m./f.,* enemy,
stranger, opponent

hūmānus, -a, -um, *adj.,* human

humilis, -e, *adj.,* low, slight

iaceō, -ēre, iacuī, —, to lie
down, recline at dinner

iactō (1), to throw, cast; *reflex.:*
boast

iactūra, -ae, *f.,* throwing away,
loss

iam, *adv.,* now; already + *pres.;*
soon + *fut.*

iānitor, -ōris, *m.,* doorkeeper,
porter

iānua, -ae, *f.,* door

Idaeus, -a, -um, *adj.,* of Mt. Ida,
where Jupiter was raised

īdem, eadem, idem, *pron.,* the
same

igitur, *adv.,* then, therefore,
accordingly

ignis, -is, *m.,* fire

ignōscō, -ere, -nōvī, -nōtum, to
overlook, forgive + *dat.*

Iliacus, -a, -um, *adj.,* of Ilium,
Trojan

Ilias, Iliadis, *f.,* the *Iliad*
(Homer's epic poem in
Greek)

ille, illa, illud, *pron.,* he, she,
it; that

illīc, *adv.,* in that place, there

illūdō, -ere, -lūsī, -lūsum, to
mock; play with, trifle away

imbēcillus, -a, -um, *adj.,* weak,
feeble

imber, -bris, *m.,* rain, shower

imitor, -ārī, -ātus sum, to copy,
mimic

imperium, -ī, *n.,* dominion,
empire

imperō (1), to command,
control + *dat.*

impleō. *See* **inpleō**

improbus. *See* **inprobus**

īmus, -a, -um, *adj.,* deepest,
lowest

in, *prep.* + *acc. or abl.,* into,
toward, with respect to; in

inānis, -e, *adj.,* empty

incendium, -ī, *n.,* fire

incendō, -ere, -cendī, -cēnsum,
to set on fire, kindle

incolumis, -e, *adj.,* unharmed,
safe

inde, *adv.,* from this place,
thence

indigena, -ae, *adj.,* native,
indigenous

indignātiō, -ōnis, *f.,*
indignation, anger

indormiō, -īre, -īvī, -ītum, to
sleep on or over

indu, *prep.* + *acc. or abl.,* rare
early form of **in**

indūcō, -ere, -dūxī, -ductum,
to lead in

indulgeō, -ēre, -dūlsī, -ultum,
to show favor to, concede to
+ *dat.*

iners, *gen.* **-ertis,** *adj.,* indolent,
sluggish

īnfāmis, -e, *adj.,* disreputable

īnfāns, -antis, *m./f.,* child,
infant

īnfāns, *gen.* **-antis,** *adj.,* mute;
infant, young

infēlīx, *gen.* **-īcis,** *adj.,*
unfortunate, unhappy

īnfernus, -a, -um, *adj.,* lower; of
the underworld

īnfitior, -ārī, -ātus sum, to
disavow, deny

īnfodiō, -ere, -fōdī, -fōssum, to
bury, inter

infrā, *adv.,* underneath, on the
underside

inhibeō, -ēre, -uī, -itum, to
restrain, prevent

inhiō (1), to gape, gaze longingly

inhonestus, -a, -um, *adj.,*
shameful, degrading

inimīcus, -a, -um, *adj.,*
unfriendly, hostile

inīquus, -a, -um, *adj.,* unequal

inmemor, *gen.* **-oris,** *adj.,*
forgetful, heedless

inmēnsus, *adj.,* boundless, vast

inops, *gen.* **-opis,** *adj.,* destitute,
poor; contemptible

inpellō, -ere, -pulī, -pulsum, to
push, push against

inpēnsa, -ae, *f.,* expense;
building materials

inpleō, -ēre, -ēvī, -ētum, to fill
up

inprobitās, -ātis, *f.,* depravity,
dishonesty

inprobus, -a, -um, *adj.,*
shameless, bold, reckless

inprūdēns, *gen.* **-entis,** *adj.,*
unaware, ignorant

inpūne, *adv.,* without
punishment, without risk

inquam, inquis, inquit, *fut.*
inquiēs, inquiet, *defective*
verb, to say

īnsāniō, -īre, -īvī, -ītum, to be
mad, be unsound

īnscrībō, -ere, -scrīpsī,
-scrīptum, to trace lines
upon, score

īnsector, -ārī, -ātus sum, to
pursue, attack furiously

īnsīdīae, -ārum, *f.pl.,* ambush,
treachery

īnsidiātor, -ōris, *m.,* one who
lies in ambush

īnsigne, -is, *n.,* distinguishing
mark; token, decoration

insistō, -ere, -stitī, to stand in
or on + *dat.*

īnstituō, -ere, -uī, -ūtum, to
establish, set up; instruct;
establish a practice

īnsuēscō, -ere, -suēvī, -suētum,
to accustom to, habituate to

īnsum, inesse, īnfuī, —, to be
in or on

intendō, -ere, -tendī, -tentum,
to stretch; direct; endeavor

inter, *prep.* + *acc.,* among

intereā, *adv.,* meanwhile

intestātus, -a, -um, *adj.,* intestate

intorqueō, -ēre, -torsī,
-tortum, to twist, distort

intrā, *prep.* + *acc.,* within

intrōrsum, *adv.,* inwardly,
within

inūtilis, -e, *adj.,* unprofitable,
harmful

inveniō, -īre, -vēnī, -ventum,
find, discover

iocus, -ī, *m.,* joke; object of mockery

Īonius, -a, -um, *adj.* Ionian; (*in n. sing., sc.* **mare**) the Ionian sea (*to the west of Greece*)

ipse, ipsa, ipsum, *pron.,* himself/herself/itself

īra, -ae, *f.,* anger, wrath

īrātus, -a, -um, *adj.,* angry, enraged, violent

is, ea, id, *pron.,* he, she, it; this, that

iste, ista, istud, *pron.,* that, that of yours

istinc, *adv.,* from that place, thence; from that source

ita, *adv.* in this manner, thus, so

Italus, -a, -um, *adj.,* Italian

item, *adv.,* likewise

iter, itineris, *n.,* journey, road

iterum, *adv.,* again, a second time

iubeō, -ēre, iūssī, iūssum, to order, bid, invite

Iudaeī, -ōrum, *m. pl.,* the Jews

iūdex, -icis, *m./f.,* judge

iūgerum, -ī, *n.,* measure of land, acre

iugulum, -ī, *n.,* throat

iugum, -ī, *n.,* ridge

iūnīx, -īcis, *f.,* young cow, heifer

Iuno, -onis, *f.,* Juno, queen of the gods

Iuppiter, Iovis, *m.,* Jupiter or Jove, king of the gods

iūs, iūris, *n.,* broth, gravy

iūs, iūris, *n.,* law, right

iūstus, -a, -um, *adj.,* just, fair

iuvenis, -is, *m.,* young man, youth

iuvō, -āre, iūvī, iūtum, to help, aid; delight, please

labellum, -ī, *n.,* little lip

Labeō, -ōnis, *m.,* Labeo, a poet

labō (1), to totter, give way

lābor, -ī, lapsus sum, to glide, slip, slip away

labōrō (1), to labor, take pains

labrum, -ī, *n.,* lip

lāc, lactis, *n.,* milk

lacerna, -ae, *f.,* cloak, mantle

lacerta, -ae, *f.,* lizard

laetus, -a, -um, *adj.,* happy; rejoicing in + *abl.*

Lāgus, -ī, *m.,* Lagus, an Egyptian king

Lamia, -ae, *f.,* Lamia, a mythical witch

lānūgō, -inis, *f.,* down, woolliness

lapillus, -ī, *m.,* small stone

lapis, -idis, *m.,* stone

lār, laris, *m.,* household; (*in pl.*) Lares, guardian gods of the household

Larga, -ae, *f.,* Larga, a woman's name

largiter, *adv.,* in abundance, very much

lascīvus, -a, -um, *adj.,* playful, wanton

lātē, *adv.,* broadly, widely

lateō, -ēre, -uī, —, to lie hidden, lurk

lātus, -a, -um, *adj.,* broad, wide

laudō (1), to praise, approve

Laureolus, -ī, *m.*, Laureolus, a character in a mime

laurus, -ī, *f.*, laurel, laurel crown

lautus, -a, -um, *adj.*, elegant, fashionable; sumptuous, rich

laxō (1), to make loose, release

lēctor, -ōris, *m.*, reader

lectulus, -ī, *m.*, small couch for reclining

lectus, -ī, *m.*, bed, couch

Lēda, -ae, *f.*, Leda, mother of Helen in myth

legō, -ere, lēgī, lēctum, to read

lēniter, *adv.*, softly, smoothly

lēnō, -ōnis, *m.*, pimp, brothel-keeper

Lentulus, -ī, *m.*, Lentulus, member of a noble family

levis, -e, *adj.*, light; weak, fickle

libellus, -ī, *m.*, small book

libenter, *adv.*, willingly, with pleasure

liber, -brī, *m.*, book

līber, -era, -erum, *adj.*, free; free-speaking, open

libet, -ere, libuit, libitum est, it pleases, it is agreeable to + *dat. and inf.*

libīdō, -inis, *f.*, lust, longing

lībō (1), to pour, sprinkle; offer sacrifice

Lībra, -ae, *f.*, Libra, the constellation representing a scale or balance

licet, -ēre, licuit *or* **licitum est,** it is allowed + *dat. and subjunctive*; although + *subjunctive*

Licinus, -ī, *m.*, Licinus, a wealthy freedman of Julius Caesar

līmen, -inis, *n.*, threshold, doorway

līmus, -ī, *m.*, mud

lingua, -ae, *f.*, tongue

linteum, -ī, *n.*, linen napkin, towel

Liparaeus, -a, -um, *adj.*, of Lipare, an island north of Sicily

liquēscō, -ere, —, —, to melt, dissolve

liquidum, -ī, *n.*, liquid, water

littera, -ae, *f.*, letter (*of the alphabet*)

locō (1), to hire out

loculus, -ī, *m.*, receptacle; money-box

locuplēs, *gen.* **-ētis,** *adj.*, rich, wealthy

locus, -ī, *m.*, place, site; rank, position

longē, *adv.*, far off, at a distance

longius, *compar. adv.*, longer, for a longer time

longus, -a, -um, *adj.*, long

loquor, -ī, locūtus sum, to speak, talk

lucerna, -ae, *f.*, lamp, oil lamp

Lūcilius, -ī, *m.*, Lucilius, the first Roman satirist

Lucusta, -ae, *f.*, Lucusta, a poisoner who lived during the reign of Nero

lūdō, -ere, lūsī, lūsum, to play, jest; mock; gamble

lūdus, -ī, *m.*, (*in sing.*) company of gladiators; (*in pl.*) games

lūmen, -inis, *n.*, light, glow, brightness

Lupus, -ī, *m.*, L. Cornelius Lentulus Lupus, a target of Lucilius' *Satires*

luscus, -a, -um, *adj.*, one-eyed

lūstrālis, -e, *adj.*, lustral, of purification

lūstrō (1), to purify with sacrifice

lutum, -ī, *n.*, mud

luxuria, -ae, *f.*, extravagance

macer, -cra, -crum, *adj.*, skinny, lean

Macrīnus, -ī, *m.*, Macrinus, a man's name (*addressee of Persius*)

macula, -ae, *f.*, stain, blot

Maecēnas, -ae, *m.*, Maecenas, patron of Horace

magis, *compar. adv.*, more, rather

magister, -trī, *m.*, teacher

magnus, -a, -um, *adj.*, great, large; important

māior, -us, *compar. adj.*, greater, larger

māiōrēs, -um, *m.pl.*, ancestors, forefathers

male, *adv.*, badly, wrongly; insufficiently, not at all

mālō *or* **māvōlō, mālle, māluī,** —, to wish, choose, prefer

malus, -a, -um, *adj.*, bad, evil, wicked

Mamercī, -ōrum, *m.pl.*, the Mamerci, a noble family

mandō (1), to entrust, commit to one's charge

māne, *adv.*, in the morning, early; *n. with abl.* **mānī,** morning

manifestus, -a, -um, *adj.*, clear, evident, plain

manus, -ūs, *f.*, hand; band

mare, -is, *n.*, sea

marītus, -ī, *m.*, husband

marmor, -oris, *n.*, marble

marmoreus, -a, -um, *adj.*, of marble

mās, maris, *m.*, man, male

māter, -tris, *f.*, mother, matron

māteria, -ae, *f.*, stuff, matter

māternus, -a, -um, *adj.*, maternal, a mother's

mātertera, -ae, *f.*, maternal aunt

mātrōna, -ae, *f.*, married woman, wife

mediocris, -e, *adj.*, average, ordinary

medius, -a, -um, *adj.*, mid; in the middle

Megalēsia, -ium, *n.pl.*, spring festival for the goddess Cybele

mēiō, -ere, —, —, to urinate

Melanippē, -ēs, *f.*, Melanippe, a character in myth and tragedy

melior, -ius, *compar. adj.*, better

melius, *adv.*, better

membrum, -ī, *n.*, limb

meminī, -isse, *defective verb*, to remember, recollect

memorō (1), to mention, tell of

mēns, mentis, *f.*, mind, sense

mēnsa, -ae, f., table

Mercurius, -ī, m., Mercury, son of Jupiter and god of wealth

mereō, -ēre, -uī, -itum, or mereor, -ērī, -itus sum, to earn, win

meretrīcula, -ae, f., prostitute (diminutive or derogatory)

meretrīx, -īcis, f., prostitute

mergō, -ere, mērsī, mērsum, to dip, immerse

meritō, adv., deservedly, with good reason

merum, -ī, n., unmixed wine, wine without water

mēta, -ae, f., mark, cone

metuō, -ere, -uī, -ūtum, to fear

metus, -ūs, m., fear, dread, anxiety

meus, -a, -um, possessive pron., my

mīlia, -ium, adj., pl. of mille

mille, adj., one thousand

mīmus, -ī, m., mime-actor

Minerva, -ae, f., Minerva, Roman goddess of war, crafts, and wisdom

minor, -us, compar. adj., smaller; too small

mīrē, adv., uncommonly, marvelously

mīror, -ārī, -ātus sum, to wonder or marvel at

mīrus, -a, -um, adj., astonishing, amazing

mīsceō, -ēre, mīscuī, mīxtum, to mix

miser, -era, -erum, adj., pitiful, unhappy

miserābilis, -e, adj., pitiable, miserable

mītis, -e, adj., mild, gentle

mittō, -ere, mīsī, missum, to send, launch

modicus, -a, -um, adj., moderate, ordinary

modius, -ī, m., measure, peck

modus, -ī, m., manner; measure, limit

moecha, -ae, f., adulteress

moechus, -ī, m., adulterer, debaucher

moenia, -ium, n.pl., walls

mollis, -e, adj., mild, soft; sensitive; effeminate

mons, montis, m., mountain

mōnstrō (1), to point out, show, instruct

mōnstrum, -ī, n., unnatural thing, miracle, prodigy

mordāx, gen. -ācis, adj., biting, sharp

moror, -ārī, -ātus sum, to delay, linger

mors, mortis, f., death

mōs, mōris, m., moral habit, character; custom, practice

moveō, -ēre, mōvī, mōtum, to move, stir, shake, rouse

Mūcius, -ī, m., Q. Mucius Scaevola, a target of Lucilius' Satires

mūcrō, -ōnis, m., sharp point, sword-point

mūla, -ae, f., she-mule

mulier, -eris, f., woman

multus, -a, -um, adj., great, much; many

Mulvius, -ī, *m.,* Mulvius, a man's name

mūnus, -eris, *n.,* service; show, exhibition

murmillō, -ōnis, *m.,* gladiator in Gallic arms

murmur, -uris, *n.,* murmur

murmurō (1), to murmur, mutter

mūs, mūris, *m./f.,* mouse

mūtō (1), to change, exchange

muttiō, -īre, —, -ītum, to mutter

nam, *conj.,* for

nāris, -is, *f.,* nostril, nose

nārrō (1), to relate, tell

nāsus, -ī, *m.,* nose; sense of smell, taste

natō (1), to swim, float

nātūra, -ae, *f.,* character, nature; talent; Nature

nātus, -ī, *m.,* son, child

nātus, -a, -um, *adj.,* born

nauta, -ae, *m.,* sailor, mariner

nāvigium, -ī, *n.,* ship, vessel

nāvis, -is, *f.,* ship, vessel

nē, *conj.,* that not, lest, so that not

-ne, *interr. particle, introduces a question*

nebulō, -ōnis, *m.,* worthless man, scoundrel

nec *or* **neque,** *conj.,* and not, but not, nor; **nec . . . nec,** neither . . . nor; **necne,** or not

necō (1), to kill, put to death

nectar, -aris, *n.,* nectar, the drink of the gods

nefās, *indecl. noun,* crime, sin

negō (1), refuse, deny

nēmō, *m./f.,* nobody, no one

nemorōsus, -a, -um, *adj.,* wooded

neque. *See* **nec**

nequeō, -quīre, -quīvī, -quītum, to be unable

nēquior, -ius, *compar. adj.,* more worthless

nēquīquam, *adv.,* in vain, fruitlessly

Nerius, -ī, *m.,* Nerius, a man's name

Nerō, -ōnis, *m.,* Nero, the last emperor of the Julio-Claudian dynasty

nervus, -ī, *m.,* sinew, tendon

nesciō, -īre, -īvī, —, not to know, to be ignorant

nescius, -a, -um, *adj.,* ignorant, unaware

neu, *adv.,* and not, nor, or not

nī, *conj.,* if not, unless

nīdor, -ōris, *m.,* smell, aroma

nīger, -gra, -grum, *adj.,* black

nihil *or* **nīl,** *indecl. n.,* nothing

nihilum, -ī, *n.,* nothing

nil. *See* **nihil**

Nīlus, -ī, *m.,* the Nile, Egypt's famous river

nimbus, -ī, *m.,* cloud

nīmīrum, *adv.,* without doubt, certainly

nisi, *conj.,* if not, unless

nitidus, -a, -um, shining, bright

nix, nivis, *f.,* snow

nō (1), to swim, float

nōbilis, -e, *adj.,* noble

nōlō, nōlle, nōluī, —, to be
  unwilling, refuse, wish not
nōmen, -inis, *n.*, name
nōn, *adv.*, not, by no means, no
nōnāria, -ae, *f.*, woman who
  starts work at the ninth
  hour, i.e., a prostitute
nōndum, *adv.*, not yet
nōnne, *adv.*, is it not, surely
nōnus, -a, -um, *adj.*, ninth
nōs, *pers. pron.*, we
nōscō, -ere, nōvī, nōtum, to
  come to know; know
noster, nostra, nostrum,
  possessive pron., our, our
  own
notō (1), to mark, observe
novus, -a, -um, *adj.*, new, novel
nox, noctis, *f.*, night, darkness
nūbēs, -is, *f.*, cloud
nūdō (1), to lay bare, expose
nūdus, -a, -um, *adj.*, naked,
  bare, nude
nūgae, -ārum, *f.pl.*, trifles,
  nonsense
nūllus, -a, -um, *adj.*, not any,
  none, no
Numa, -ae, *m.*, Numa, the
  second king of Rome
nūmen, -inis, *n.*, divine will,
  divinity
numerō (1), count, take account
  of
numerus, -ī, *m.*, number
nummus, -ī, *m.*, cash; coin
numquam, *adv.*, at no time,
  never
numquid, *adv.*, surely not, is it
  possible

nunc, *adv.*, now
nūpta, -ae, *f.*, bride; wife of +
  dat.
nurus, -ūs, *f.*, daughter-in-law
nūsquam, *adv.*, nowhere, in no
  place
nūtrīx, -īcis, *f.*, nurse
nux, nucis, *f.*, nut

ō, *interj.*, oh!
obdūrō (1), to persist, endure
obiciō, -ere, -iēcī, -iectum, to
  hold up, present
obscūrō (1), to cover, conceal
obsequium, -ī, *n.*, servility,
  indulgence
obstō, -stāre, -stitī, —, to
  obstruct, stand in the way of
  + *dat.*
obvolvō, -ere, -volvī, -volūtum,
  to wrap up, cover over
occidō, -ere, -cīdī, -cāsum, to
  kill, strike or cut down
occurrō, -ere, -currī, -cursum,
  to come across, meet
ōcius, *compar. adv.*, quickly,
  more quickly
oculus, -ī, *m.*, eye
ōdī, ōdisse, *defective verb*, to
  hate, condemn
odium, -ī, *n.*, hatred, ill will
odōrātus, -a, -um, *adj.*,
  perfumed
officiōsus, -a, -um, *adj.*, ready
  to serve, obliging
olētum, -ī, *n.*, excrement
oleum, -ī, *n.*, oil
ōlim, *adv.*, formerly, long ago;
  one day, ever

omāsum, -ī, *n.,* tripe
ōmentum, -ī, *n.,* fat, intestine
ōmittō, -ere, -mīsī, -missum, to let go, lay aside
omnis, -e, *adj.,* all, every
onustus, -a, -um, *adj.,* laden, burdened
opera, -ae, *f.,* labor; (*by metonymy*) laborer
opertus, -a, -um, *adj.,* covered, secret
opicus, -a, -um, *adj.,* barbarous, rude
opīmus, -a, -um, *adj.,* rich, splendid
opprobrium, -ī, *n.,* reproach, scandal
ops, opis, *f.,* power, wealth
optimus, -a, -um, *superl. adj.,* best
optō (1), to choose, wish for, desire
opus, -eris, *n.,* work, labor; **opus est** + *abl.,* there is need of
orbis, -is, *m.,* disk, dish
orbita, -ae, *f.,* rut, track
orbus, -a, -um, *adj.,* childless
Orcus, -ī, *m.,* Orcus, Roman god of the dead; the underworld
Orestēs, -ae, *m.,* Orestes, son of the mythical king Agamemnon
ōrnāmentum, -ī, *n.,* ornament, embellishment
ōrnō (1), to adorn, decorate
ōs, ōris, *n.,* mouth, face
os, ossis, *n.,* bone

ostendō, -ere, -tendī, -tentum, to show, exhibit, present
ōtium, -ī, *n.,* leisure, free time
ovīle, -is, *n.,* sheepfold
ōvum, -ī, *n.,* egg

Pacideiānus, -ī, *m.,* Pacideiānus, a gladiator
pactum, -ī, *n.,* compact; manner, means
paene, *adv.,* nearly, almost
palleō, -ēre, -uī, —, to be pale, fade
pānis, -is, *m.,* bread, loaf of bread
pār, *gen.* **paris,** *adj.,* equal, like
parasītus, -ī, *m.,* parasite
parātus, -ūs, *m.,* equipment, trappings
Parca, -ae, *f.,* Parca, a goddess of Fate
parcō, -ere, pepercī, parsum, to use sparingly; refrain from harming + *dat.*
parcē, *adv.,* thriftily, economically
parēns, -entis, *m./f.,* parent; ancestor
Paris, -idis, *m.,* Paris, an actor
pariter, *adv.,* equally, together
parō (1), to prepare, get, provide; intend
pars, partis, *f.,* part, portion
parvulus, -a, -um, *adj.,* very small
parvus, -a, -um, *adj.,* small, little
pateō, -ēre, -uī, —, to be open, exposed, accessible

pater, -tris, *m.*, father, sire
paternus, -a, -um, *adj.*, of a
father, paternal
patiēns, *gen.* **-entis,** *adj.*,
tolerant, enduring
patina, -ae, *f.*, dish, flat pan
patior, -ī, passus sum, to suffer,
allow
patria, -ae, *f.*, fatherland, native
land
patricius, -a, -um, *adj.*,
patrician, aristocrat
patrimōnium, -ī, *n.*,
inheritance
patrius, -a, -um, *adj.*, of a
father; inherited
patruus, -ī, *m.*, paternal uncle
paucus, -a, -um, *adj.*, few, little
paulātim, *adv.*, little by little,
gradually
pauper, *gen.* **-eris,** *adj.*, poor, of
small means
pauperō (1), to impoverish, rob
of + *abl.*
paveō, -ēre, pāvī, —, to quake,
be frightened
pavidus, -a, -um, *adj.*, quaking,
scared
pāvō, -ōnis, *m.*, peacock
pavor, -ōris, *m.*, panic, terror
peccātum, -ī, *n.*, error, sin
peccō (1), to err, go wrong, sin
pectus, -oris, *n.*, breast, heart
pecus, -oris, *n.*, herd, flock (*of
cattle or sheep*)
pēior, -us, *compar. adj.*, worse,
more evil
pelagus, -ī, *n.*, sea
pellicula, -ae, *f.*, skin

Penātēs, -ium, *m.*, the Penates,
guardian gods of the
household; household stores
pendeō, -ēre, pependī, —, to
hang, be suspended
per, *prep.* + *acc.*, through;
according to
perdō, -ere, -didī, -ditum, to
waste, squander, lose
peregrīnus, -a, -um, *adj.*,
foreign
pereō, -īre, -iī, -itum, to perish,
be destroyed
perferō, -ferre, -tulī, -lātum, to
endure, bear
pērgula, -ae, *f.*, storefront, shop
perīculum, -ī, *n.*, danger, risk
perītus, -a, -um, *adj.*, skillful;
skilled or experienced at +
inf.
permittō, -ere, -mīsī, -missum,
to permit, allow
perniciēs, -ēī, *f.*, destruction,
ruin
pernoctō (1), to stay all night
long, to pass the night
perrārō, *adv.*, very seldom
Persicus, -ī, *m.*, Persicus, a
man's name
persolvō, -ere, -solvī,
-solūtum, to pay, pay in full
persōna, -ae, *f.*, mask
perstō, -stāre, -stitī, -stātum,
to stand firmly, persevere
pēs, pedis, *m.*, foot
pessimus, -a, -um, *superl. adj.*,
worst
petō, -ere, -īvī / -iī, -ītum, to
seek, strive after

petulāns, *gen.* **-antis**, *adj.*, saucy, impudent

Phāros, **-ī**, *f.*, Pharos, an island near Alexandria, Egypt

Phasma, **-matis**, *n.*, *Phasma*, a comic play about a ghost

pīctor, **-ōris**, *m.*, painter

pīctus, **-a**, **-um**, *adj.*, painted, decorated

pingō, **-ere**, **pīnxī**, **pīctum**, to paint

pinguis, **-e**, *adj.*, thick, heavy

piō (1), to purify, atone for

piscis, **-is**, *m.*, fish

plāga, **-ae**, *f.*, blow; stroke (*of a whip*)

plānipēs, **-pedis**, *m.*, barefoot actor, a kind of mime or ballet-dancer

planta, **-ae**, *f.*, plant, shoot

planta, **-ae**, *f.*, sole of the foot

plaudō, **-ere**, **plausī**, **plausum**, to applaud, approve

plēbēs, **-eī** *or* **plēbs**, **plēbis**, *f.*, plebeians, common people

plēnus, **-a**, **-um**, *adj.*, full, ample

plōrō (1), to lament, weep aloud

plūma, **-ae**, *f.*, feather, down

plūs, *gen.* **plūris**, *adj.*, more

Plūtōn, **-ōnis**, *m.*, Pluto, god of the underworld

pluvia, **-ae**, *f.*, rain

pōculum, **-ī**, *n.*, cup, goblet

poena, **-ae**, *f.*, punishment

poēta, **-ae**, *m.*, poet

pollex, **-icis**, *m.*, thumb

polluō, **-ere**, **-luī**, **-lūtum**, to defile, pollute

Polyclītus, **-ī**, *m.*, Polyclitus, a famous sculptor of classical Athens

Pōlydamas, **-ae**, *m.*, Polydamas, a Trojan commander in Homer's *Iliad*

Polyphēmus, **-ī**, *m.*, Polyphemus, the mythical Cyclops

Pompilius, **-ī**, *m.*, Pompilius, cognomen of **Numa**

pondus, **-eris**, *n.*, weight, burden

pōnō, **-ere**, **posuī**, **positum**, to place, put; serve; lay aside; use, dispose of

popīnō, **-ōnis**, *m.*, glutton

populus, **-ī**, *m.*, people, crowd; nation

porrigō, **-ere**, **-rēxī**, **-rēctum**, to extend, offer

porticus, **-ūs**, *f.*, colonnade, portico

portō (1), to bear, carry

pōscō, **-ere**, **popōscī**, to ask for, demand

possum, **posse** *or* **potesse**, **potuī**, —, to be able, to have power, can

post, *prep.* + *acc.*, after, following

postis, **-is**, *m.*, doorpost; door

postrēmus, **-a**, **-um**, *adj.*, last, final

potēns, *gen.* **-entis**, *adj.*, powerful

potestās, **-ātis**, *f.*, power; legal power

pōtō (1), to drink

praebeō, -ēre, -uī, -itum, to offer, provide

praecēdō, -ere, -cēssī, -cessum, to go before, precede

praecipiō, -ere, -cēpī, -ceptum, to advise, instruct

praeclārus, -a, -um, *adj.*, famous, distinguished

praecordia, -ōrum, *n.pl.*, heart, breast

praeferō, -ferre, -tulī, -lātum, to prefer, place before

praegrandis, -e, *adj.*, very large; mighty

Praeneste, -is, *f./n.*, Praeneste, a town in Latium

praenōmen, -inis, *n.*, first name, personal name

praerōdō, -ere, —, -rōsum, to gnaw at, nibble

praesēns, *gen.* **-entis,** *adj.*, at hand, prompt

praestō, -stāre, -stitī, -stitum, to show, present

praetereā, *adv.*, besides, moreover; thereafter

praetextātus, -a, -um, *adj.*, underage, teenage

praetor, -ōris, *m.*, praetor, judge, official

praetōrium, -ī, *n.*, palace, mansion

prandeō, -ēre, prandī, prānsum, to eat lunch

prandium, -ī, *n.*, luncheon

prāvus, -a, -um, *adj.*, crooked, perverse

precor, -ārī, precātus sum, to pray for

premō, -ere, pressī, pressum, to press, press closely, pursue

pretium, -ī, *n.*, price, worth

prex, -ecis, *f.*, prayer, request

prīmum, *adv.*, first, in the first place

prīmus, -a, -um, *adj.*, first, foremost, earliest

prīnceps, -cipis, *m./f.*, ruler, emperor

prior, prius, *compar. adj.*, in front, the first, fore

prius, *compar. adv.*, before, sooner

priusquam, *conj.*, before, until, sooner than

prīvātus, -a, -um, *adj.*, private, ordinary; (*as a noun*) private citizen

probitās, -ātis, *f.*, honesty

procer, -eris, *m.*, leading man, noble

procul, *adv.*, far away

Procula, -ae, *f.*, Procula, a woman's name

prōdeō, -īre, -iī, -itum, to go or come forward

prōdigiōsus, -a, -um, *adj.*, unnatural, marvelous

prōdigium, -ī, *n.*, portent, marvelous sign

proelium, -ī, *n.*, battle, combat

profēstus, -a, -um, *adj.*, not kept as a holiday, ordinary

profundum, -ī, *n.*, abyss, depth (e.g., of the underworld)

prōiciō, -ere, -iēcī, -iectum, to cast down, discard

prōmptus, -a, -um, *adj.,* ready, easy

prōnus, -a, -um, *adj.,* leaning, sloping

prope, *adv.,* nearby, close by

propinquus, -a, -um, *adj.,* near, neighboring, related

propinquus, -ī, *m.,* kinsman, relative

proprius, -a, -um, *adj.,* one's own, personal

propter, *prep. + acc.,* for the sake of, because of

prōstituō, -ere, -uī, -ūtum, to expose for sale, to prostitute

prōtinus, *adv.,* directly, straightaway

proximus, -a, -um, *superl. adj.,* nearest, next

prūdēns, *gen.* -entis, *adj.,* aware, acting deliberately

Publius, -ī, *m.,* Publius, a man's **praenomen**

pudendus, -a, -um, *adj.,* shameful, scandalous

puella, -ae, *f.,* girl, young woman; slave-girl

puer, -erī, *m.,* boy, child

pugnō (1), to fight, struggle

pulcher, -chra, -chrum, *adj.,* beautiful, fair, handsome

pullātus, -a, -um, *adj.,* clothed in black, in mourning

pulmō, -ōnis, *m.,* lung

pulpitum, -ī, *n.,* platform, stage

pulsō (1), strike, knock

pulvis, -eris, *m.,* dust, powder

pūpillus, -ī, *m.,* orphan, ward

puppis, -is, *f.,* stern of a ship

pūrgō (1), to make clean, purify

purpura, -ae, *adj.,* purple, of purple cloth

pūrus, -a, -um, *adj.,* clear, pure

pusillus, -a, -um, *adj.,* very little

puteus, -ī, *m.,* well

pūtidus, -a, -um, *adj.,* rotten, stinking

putō (1), to consider, think, estimate, imagine

Pyrrha, -ae, *f.,* Pyrrha, wife of **Deucalion** in myth

Pȳthagorēus, -a, -um, *adj.* of the philosopher Pythagorus; (*as a noun*) follower of Pythagorus

quadrivium, -ī, *n.,* cross-road

quaerō, -ere, quaesīvī *or* **quaesiī, quaesītum,** to search for, seek, ask for

quālis, -e, *rel. adj.,* of such a kind as

quāliscumque, quālecumque, *adj.,* of whatever kind

quam, *adv.,* (*in comparisons*) than

quamquam, *conj.,* although

quamvīs, *adv.,* although, however much

quandō, *adv.,* when, at what time

quandōque, *adv.,* at some time, at one time or other

quantus, -a, -um, *interr. adj.,* how great; *rel. adj.,* as great as

quārē, *adv.,* how, in what way, why

quātenus, *adv.*, inasmuch as

quatiō, -ere, —, quassum, to shake, tremble

quattuor, *indecl. adj.*, four

-que, *conj.*, and

quī, quae, quod, *rel. pron.*, who, which

quia, *conj.*, because

quīcumque, quaecumque, quodcumque, *rel. pron.*, whoever, whatever; any

quid, *interr. adv.*, why

quīdam, quaedam, quoddam, *indef. pron.*, someone, something, a certain

quīngentī, -ae, -a, five hundred

Quintiliānus, -ī, *m.*, Quintilian, a famous rhetorician

Quintus, -ī, *m.*, Quintus, a man's **praenomen**

quippe, *conj.*, certainly; for in fact

quis, quid, *interr. pron.*, who, which, what; *indef. pron.*, any; *after* **si, nisi, num, ne,** *equivalent to* **aliquis, aliquid**

quisquam, quaequam, quicquam, *indef. pron.*, anyone, anything

quisque, quaeque, quidque, *indef. pron.*, each, every

quisquis, quidquid, *indef. pron.*, whoever, whatever

quīvīs, quaevīs, quidvīs, *indef. pron.*, whoever it be, whatever it be, any whatever

quō, *adv. and conj.*, to which place, to which purpose; at which time, when

quōcumque, *adv.*, wherever, to whatever place

quod, *conj.*, because; the fact that

quondam, *adv.*, formerly, at one time

quoniam, *adv.*, since, because

quoque, *adv.*, also, too

quōrsum, *adv.*, in what direction, to what purpose or end

quotiēns, *adv.*, as many times as, whenever

rādō, -ere, rāsī, rāsum, to scrape, peel

rāmōsus, -a, -um, *adj.*, branching, forked

rapiō, -ere, rapuī, raptum, to seize, carry off; snatch at

rāstrum, -ī, *n.*, toothed hoe

ratiō, -ōnis, *f.*, reason, grounds

recēssus, -ūs, *m.*, retreat, secret spot

recondō, -ere, -condidī, -conditum, to put back again, stow away

rēctē, *adv.*, correctly, properly

rēctus, -a, -um, *adj.*, right, proper, honest

recubō (1), to lie back, recline

recūsō (1), to refuse, be reluctant

reddō, -ere, -didī, -ditum, to give, give back; duly give

redigō, -ere, -ēgī, -āctum, to bring back, reduce, render

referō, -ferre, rettulī, relātum, to recall, mention

rēfert, -ferre, rētulit, —, make a difference, matter

rēgīna, -ae, *f.*, queen

rēgula, -ae, *f.*, bar; rule, model

relinquō, -ere, -līquī, -lictum, to leave behind, leave; allow (+ *dat. and inf.*)

reliquus, -a, -um, *adj.*, remaining

renāscor, -ī, renātus sum, to grow again

repōnō, -ere, -posuī, -positum, to return, put back, replace

requiēs, -ētis, *f.*, rest, relaxation

rēs, reī, *f.*, thing, matter, circumstance; case; property, material wealth

resignō (1), to unseal, reveal

respīrō (1), to take a breath

restis, -is, *f.*, rope

rēticulum, -ī, *n.*, net bag

reverentia, -ae, *f.*, respect, reverence

rēx, rēgis, *m.*, ruler, king

rīdeō, -ēre, rīsī, rīsum, to laugh, laugh at

rīma, -ae, *f.*, crack, fissure

rīpa, -ae, *f.*, bank of a stream

rīsus, -ūs, *m.*, laugh, smile

rōdō, -ere, rōsī, rōsum, to gnaw, eat away

rogō (1), to ask, beg, request

Rōma, -ae, *f.*, Rome; *locative* **Rōmae**

Rōmānus, -a, -um, *adj.*, Roman

rosa, -ae, *f.*, rose

rota, -ae, *f.*, wheel; circular rack (*instrument of torture*)

ruber, -bra, -brum, *adj.*, red, ruddy

rubēta, -ae, *f.*, toad

rudēns, -entis, *m.*, rope, rigging

rudis, -e, *adj.*, new, unskilled

ruīna, -ae, *f.*, ruin, falling down

rūmor, -ōris, *m.*, rumor, gossip

rumpō, -ere, rūpī, ruptum, to break

rūs, rūris, *n.*, country

rūsticus, -a, -um, *adj.*, rustic, naive

Rutilus, -ī, *m.*, Rutilus, a man's name

Sabīnus, -a, -um, *adj.*, Sabine, of Sabinum (*region northeast of Latium*)

saccus, -ī, *m.*, sack, bag

sacer, sacra, sacrum, *adj.*, sacred, consecrated

sacra, -ōrum, *n.*, holy things, sacred objects

saepe, *adv.*, often, frequently

saeviō, -īre, -iī, -ītum, to be fierce, to rage

saevus, -a, -um, *adj.*, violent, barbarous

sagitta, -ae, *f.*, arrow

salīva, -ae, *f.*, saliva, spittle

saltō (1), to dance, represent through a dance

Samnīs, *gen.* **-itis,** *adj.*, Samnite, of Samnium (*region in the central southern Apennine mountains*)

sānctē, *adv.*, conscientiously, piously

sānctus, -a, -um, *adj.,* abiding by oaths, morally pure

sanguis, -inis, *m.,* blood

sānus, -a, -um, *adj.,* healthy, sensible, safe

sapiēns, -entis, *m.,* wise man, philosopher

sapiō, -ere, sapīvī *or* **sapiī, —,** to taste of, have a flavor of

satis, *adj. and adv.,* enough

satius, *compar. adj.,* better, preferable

Sātūrnus, -ī, *m.,* Saturn, ancient king of the gods and father of Jupiter

saxum, -ī, *n.,* rock, stone

scabiōsus, -a, -um, *adj.,* scabby, mangy

scēna, -ae, *f.,* stage, show

Scētānus, -ī, *m.,* Scetanus, a man's name

sciō, -īre, scīvī, scitum, to know, understand

scrībō, -ere, scrīpsī, scrīptum, to write, compose

scrobis, -is, *m.,* ditch

scurra, -ae, *f.,* buffoon

sē *or* **sēsē,** *reflex. pron.,* himself, herself, itself, themselves

secō, -āre, secuī, sectum, to cut, cleave, divide

sēcrētē, *adv.,* without witnesses, secretly

secundus, -a, -um, *adj.,* second

sēcūrus, -a, -um, *adj.,* free from care, safe

sēd *or* **sed,** *conj.,* but, but also, however, but in fact

sēdō (1), to sit

sēdūcō, -ere, -dūxī, -ductum, to lead away, draw aside

segmentātus, -a, -um, *adj.,* trimed with fabric, flounced

sēligō, -ere, -lēgī, -lēctum, to pick out, choose

semel, *adv.,* once, a single time

semper, *adv.,* always, ever

senātor, -ōris, *m.,* senator

senecta, -ae, *f.,* old age

senectūs, -ūtis, *f.,* old age

senex, senis, *m.,* old man

sentīna, -ae, *f.,* bilge-water, scum

sentiō, -īre, sēnsī, sēnsum, to feel, think

septimus, -a, -um, *adj.,* seventh

sequor, -ī, secūtus sum, to follow, accompany

sēria, -ae, *f.,* large earthenware jar

sērius, -a, -um, *adj.,* grave, serious

sērus, -a, -um, *adj.,* late, last-minute

servō (1), to preserve, keep

servus, -ī, *m.,* slave

sēstertia, -ōrum, *n.,* one thousand sesterces (*small silver coins*)

seu. *See* **sīve**

sex, *indecl. adj.,* six

sextārius, -ī, *m.,* one-sixth of a large liquid measure; a pint

sextus, -a, -um, *adj.,* sixth

sī, *conj.,* if; if only

sībilō (1), to hiss, whistle at

sīc, *adv.,* thus, so, in this way

siccō (1), to dry up, drain

Siculus, -a, -um, *adj.* Sicilian, of the island of Sicily

sīcut, *adv.*, just as

sīdus, -eris, *n.*, constellation, star

signātor, -ōris, *m.*, signer, legal witness

signum, -ī, *n.*, statue

silva, -ae, *f.*, forest, wood

similis, -e, *adj.*, similar; like + *dat.*

simplex, *gen.* **-icis,** *adj.*, traditional, simple

simul, *adv.*, at the same time, together; **simul ac,** as soon as

simulō (1), to imitate, pretend

sine, *prep.* + *abl.*, without

sinister, -tra, -trum, *adj.*, on the left side; unfavorable, bad

sinuōsus, -a, -um, *adj.*, full of folds or recesses

sinus, -ūs, *m.*, fold, lap

sīparium, -ī, *n.*, curtain, screen in a theater

Sīrēn, -ēnis, *f.*, Siren, a mythical singing monster

sistō, -ere, stitī, statum, to cause to stand, set in place

sitiēns, *gen.* **-entis,** *adj.*, parching, thirsting

sīve *or* **seu,** *conj.*, or if, or; **sive . . . sive,** whether . . . or

Sōcraticus, -a, -um, *adj.*, of Socrates, Socratic

sōl, sōlis, *m.*, sun; day

soleō, -ēre, —, solitum, to be accustomed, be in the habit

solidus, -a, -um, *adj.*, solid, sound

sollers, *gen.* **-ertis,** *adj.*, skilled, expert

sollicitus, -a, -um, *adj.*, concerned, anxious

sōlus, -a, -um, *adj.*, only, sole

solvō, -ere, solvī, solūtum, to unloose, unbind

somnium, -ī, *n.*, dream, vision

somnus, -ī, *n.* sleep

sonō, -āre, sonuī, sonitum, to make a noise, sound

Sōra, -ae, *f.*, Sora, a town in Latium

sordēs, -is, *f.*, filth; meanness

sordidus, -a, -um, *adj.*, miserly, vulgar

soror, -ōris, *f.*, sister

sors, sortis, *f.*, lot, oracle

sortior, sortīrī, sortītus sum, to obtain by lot

spargō, -ere, spārsī, spārsum, to scatter, spread

Spartānus, -a, -um, *adj.*, Spartan, of Sparta

spectāculum, -ī, *n.*, show, spectacle

spectō (1), to watch, behold

spernō, -ere, sprēvī, sprētum, to reject, spurn

spērō (1), to hope for, look for

spēs, speī, *f.*, hope, expectation

splēn, -nis, *m.*, spleen

spōnsa, -ae, *f.*, bride, betrothed

spurcus, -a, -um, *adj.*, unclean, filthy; cruel

statua, -ae, *f.*, statue, image

stō, stāre, stetī, statum, to stand

stomachus, -ī, *m.*, gullet, stomach; ill-temper

strepitus, -ūs, *m.,* din, crashing

strīdor, -ōris, *m.,* grating, creaking

struō, -ere, struxī, structum, to pile up, build

studium, -ī, *n.,* eagerness, zeal

stultus, -a, -um, *adj.,* foolish, stupid

stupeō, -ēre, -uī, —, to be astounded, stunned

stupidus, -a, -um, *adj.,* astounded; doltish

suādeō, -ēre, suāsī, suāsum, to urge, suggest to + *dat.*

suāvis, -e, *adj.,* sweet, pleasant

sub, *prep.* + *acc. or abl.,* under; just before, up to; beneath, below

subcingō, -ere, -cīnxī, -cīnctum, to gird, tuck up

subeō, -īre, -iī, -itum, to come or go up, enter into

subitō, *adv.,* suddenly

subitus, -a, -um, *adj.,* sudden

subligar, -āre, *n.,* loincloth

Subūra, -ae, *f.,* the Subura, a neighborhood in Rome

sum, esse, fuī, futūrum, to be, exist, happen

summus, -a, -um, *adj.,* highest, uppermost, extreme

sūmō, -ere, sūmpsī, sūmptum, to take up

super, *prep.* + *acc.,* above

superī, -ōrum, *m.pl.,* those on high, the gods

supernus, -a, -um, *adj.,* on top, above

supersum, -esse, -fuī, -futūrum, to remain

supīnor, -ārī, -ātus sum, to tilt back

supīnus, -a, -um, *adj.,* face-upwards; sprawling, lying on one's back

supplex, *gen.* **-icis,** *adj.,* of a supplicant, begging

suppōnō, -ere, -posuī, -positum, to place under, set under, subject to

surdus, -a, -um, *adj.,* deaf; dull

suscipiō, -ere, -cēpī, -ceptum, to support, take up

suspectus, -a, -um, *adj.,* mistrusted, suspected

suspendō, -ere, -pendī, -pēnsum, to hang

suspīrō (1), to sigh

susurrus, -ī, *m.,* whispering, low murmur

suus, -a, -um, *pron.,* his, her, one's own

syrma, -atis, *n.,* robe with a train

tabella, -ae, *f.,* small board, painting

taberna, -ae, *f.,* booth, shop

tabula, -ae, *f.,* board; writing-tablet, document

tabulātum, -ī, *n.,* floor, storey

tacitus, -a, -um, *adj.,* silent, mute

tālis, -e, *adj.,* such, of such kind

tam, *adv.,* so, such, to such an extent

tamen, *adv.,* nevertheless, all the same, but

tamquam, *adv.*, just as, as though

tangō, -ere, tetigī, tāctum, to touch

Tantalus, -ī, *m.*, Tantalus, a mythical king who was punished in the underworld

tantulus, -a, -um, *adj.*, so little, as little as

tantum, *adv.*, to such a degree, only

tantundem, *adv.*, just as much, only so much

tantus, -a, -um, *adj.*, so great, so much, as much as

tēctōrium, -ī, *n.*, plaster, stucco

tēctum, -ī, *n.*, roof, shelter

tegō, -ere, texī, tēctum, to cover

tēgula, -ae, *f.*, roof-tiles

temperō (1), to control, temper

templum, -ī, *n.*, temple, shrine

tempus, -oris, *n.*, time, period of time

tenāx, *gen.* **-ācis,** *adj.*, holding fast, gripping

tendō, -ere, tetendī, tentum, to stretch, distend; strive, aim

tenebrae, -ārum, *f.pl.*, darkness; gloomy place

teneō, -ēre, tenuī, —, to hold fast, keep, master

tener, -era, -erum, *adj.*, tender, delicate

tenuis, -e, *adj.*, thin, fine

ter, *adv.*, three times, thrice

tergeō, -ēre, tērsī, tērsum, to wipe off

terō, -ere, trīvī, trītum, to thresh out, yield

terra, -ae, *f.*, earth, ground

terreō, -ēre, -uī, -itum, to frighten, scare

terricula, -ōrum, *n.pl.*, means of frightening; scarecrow

tertius, -a, -um, *adj.*, third

testāmentum, -ī, *n.*, will, testament

testūdineus, -a, -um, *adj.*, made of or inlaid with tortoiseshell

theātrum, -ī, *n.*, theater, play-house

Thyestēs, -ae, *m.*, Thyestes, a mythical king and character in tragedy

Thymelē, -ēs, *f.*, Thymele, an actress

thynnus, -ī, *m.*, tunny-fish

thyrsus, -ī, *m.*, wand, staff

Tiberīnus, -a, -um, *adj.*, of the Tiber river in Latium

tībīcen, -inis, *m.*, pipe; prop, strut

Tībur, -uris, *n.*, Tibur, a town in Latium

timeō, -ēre, -uī, —, to fear, dread

timidus, -a, -um, *adj.*, fearful, faint-hearted

timor, -ōris, *m.*, fear

Tītan, -ānis, *m.*, Titan (*one of an early race of gods*)

tollō, -ere, sustulī, sublātum, to lift up, raise up; draw from; take up, acknowledge (*a newborn child*), exalt

torrēns, *gen.* **-entis,** *adj.*, seething, rushing

tortor, -ōris, *m.*, torturer

torus, -ī, *m.*, couch

torvus, -a, -um, *adj.*, fierce, grim

tot, *indecl. adj.*, so many, such a number

totidem, *indecl. adj.*, just as many

totiēns, *adv.*, so often, so many times

tōtus, -a, -um, *adj.*, the whole, entire

tractō (1), to pull, handle

trādō, -ere, -didī, -ditum, to hand over, bequeath

tragoedus, -ī, *m.*, tragic actor

trahō, -ere, traxī, tractum, to draw out, pull along

trānseō, -īre, -iī, -itum, to pass by

trānsferō, -ferre, -tulī, -lātum, to carry over, carry along

Trebōnius, -ī, *m.*, Trebonius, a man's name

tremō, -ere, -uī, —, to quake; tremble at

tremulus, -a, -um, *adj.*, shaking, quaking

trepidō (1), to be panicked or anxious, scurry

trepidus, -a, -um, *adj.*, agitated, anxious

triscurria, -ōrum, *n.pl.*, gross buffooneries

tristis, -e, *adj.*, melancholy, somber, grim, gloomy

Trōias, -iados *or* **-iadis,** *f.*, a woman of Troy

Trōicus, -a, -um, *adj.*, of or concerning Troy; (*as a n.pl. noun*) a poem on the Trojan War

trutina, -ae, *f.*, balance, pair of scales

tū, *pers. pron.*, you

tūber, -eris, *n.*, truffle

tuccētum, -ī, *n.*, sausage

Tuccia, -ae, *f.*, Tuccia, a woman's name

tueor, -ērī, tūtus sum, to watch over, protect

tum, *adv.*, then, next, at that time, moreover

tumeō, -ēre, —, —, to swell, be bloated

tunc, *adv.*, then, at that time

tunica, -ae, *f.*, tunic, jacket

turba, -ae, *f.*, crowd, throng

turbidus, -a, -um, *adj.*, disordered, frantic, turbulent

turbō (1), to throw into confusion, disturb, make turbid

turgeō, -ēre, —, —, to swell out, become swollen

turgidus, -a, -um, *adj.*, swollen, inflated

turpis, -e, *adj.*, foul, filthy, disreputable

turpiter, *adv.*, in an unsightly manner, disgracefully

Tuscus, -a, -um, *adj.*, Tuscan, Etruscan (*of Etruria, northwest of Latium*)

tuus, -a, -um, *adj.*, your

tyrannis, *gen.* **-idis,** *adj.*, despotic rule, tyranny

Tyrrhēnus, -a, -um, *adj.*, of the Tyrrhenian sea (*off Italy's west coast*)

ūber, *gen.* **-eris,** *adj.*, rich,
   plentiful, fruitful
ubi, *adv.*, where, in which place;
   when
ubīque, *adv.*, everywhere,
   anywhere
Ūcalegōn, -ōnis, *m.*, Ucalegon,
   a character from epic
ūdus, -a, -um, *adj.*, moist,
   damp
ulcīscor, -ī, ultus sum, to
   avenge, take vengeance for
ultimus, -a, -um, *superl. adj.*,
   last, final, extreme
ultor, -ōris, *m.*, avenger,
   punisher
ultrō, *adv.*, moreover,
   in addition; without
   provocation
umbō, -ōnis, *m.*, protuberance;
   fold of a toga on the chest
umbra, -ae, *f.*, shade; ghost
umerus, -ī, *m.*, shoulder
ūnā, *adv.*, together
unda, -ae, *f.*, water, wave
unde, *adv.*, from which place,
   from which source, whence
undique, *adv.*, on all sides,
   everywhere
ūnus, -a, -um, *adj.*, one, single
Urbicus, -ī, *m.*, Urbicus, an
   actor
urbs, urbis, *f.*, city; Rome
urceolus, -ī, *m.*, little pitcher,
   water pot
urgeō, -ēre, ūrsī, —, to press,
   push on
urna, -ae, *f.*, urn, water-jar
ūrō, -ere, ūssī, ūstum, to burn

ūsquam, *adv.*, anywhere
ūsque, *adv.*, continuously, all
   the way
ūsus, -ūs, *m.*, use, benefit
ut *or* **utī,** *adv.*, how; +
   indicative, just as; **ut sī** +
   subjunctive, as if; *conj.*, +
   subjunctive, so that, in order
   that
uter, utra, utrum, *interr. pron.*,
   which of two; *indef. pron.*,
   whichever of the two
ūtilis, -e, *adj.*, useful, profitable
utinam, *adv.*, if only, would
   that
ūtor, -ī, ūsus sum, to make use
   of
ūva, -ae, *f.*, cluster, bunch
uxor, -ōris, *f.*, wife

vacuum, -ī, *n.*, empty space,
   void
vacuus, -a, -um, *adj.*, empty
vadimōnium, -ī, *n.*, security,
   bail
vafer, -fra, -frum, *adj.*, sly,
   crafty, subtle
valeō, -ēre, -uī, -itūrum, to be
   strong, well
validus, -a, -um, *adj.*, strong,
   robust
vapōrō (1), to fill with vapor or
   steam
-ve, *conj.*, or
vehō, -ere, vexī, vectum, to
   carry, bear
vel, *conj. and adv.*, if you will;
   or perhaps; **vel . . . vel,** either
   . . . or

vellō, -ere, vellī, vulsum, to pluck, pull

velocius, *compar. adv.,* more swiftly

vēlōx, *gen.* **-ōcis,** *adj.,* swift, quick

velut *or* **velutī,** *adv.,* just as, as if

vēnālis, -e, *adj.,* for sale

vēndō, -ere, vēndidī, vēnditum, to sell

venerābilis, -e, *adj.,* worthy of respect, venerable

venia, -ae, *f.,* favor, indulgence, pardon

veniō, -īre, vēnī, ventum, to come, arrive

venter, -tris, *m.,* stomach, belly

venus, -eris, *f.,* sexual love

(verber), verberis (*sing. only appears in gen. and abl.*), blow, strike, lash

verbum, -ī, *n.,* word

verēcundus, -a, -um, *adj.,* modest

Verginius, -ī, *m.,* L. Verginius Rufus, a provincial governor in 68 CE

vērō, *adv.,* in fact, but

versō (1), to engage oneself, be busy

versus, -ūs, *m.,* line of verse, poetry

vertex, icis, *m.,* eddy, strong current

vertō, -ere, vertī, versum, to turn around

vērum, -ī, *n.,* truth

vērum, *adv.,* truly, but

vērus, -a, -um, *adj.,* true, real

vēsīca, -ae, *f.,* bladder

vestīgium, -ī, *n.,* footstep, track

vetō, -āre, -uī, -itum, to forbid, prohibit

vetulus, -a, -um, *adj.,* wretchedly or pitiably old

vetus, *gen.* **veteris,** *adj.,* old, ancient

vīcīnus, -a, -um, *adj.,* nearby, neighboring

vīcus, -ī, *m.,* street, lane

videō, -ēre, vīdī, vīsum, to see

vigilō (1), to keep awake, be vigilant

vīlicus, -ī, *m.,* overseer, manager

vīlis, -e, *adj.,* cheap

vinciō, -īre, vīnxī, vīnctum, to bind, fetter

vincō, -ere, vīcī, victum, to overcome, defeat, conquer

Vindex, -icis, *m.,* G. Iulius Vindex, a provincial governor who revolted against Nero

vīnum, -ī, *n.,* wine

vir, virī, *m.,* man; husband

virga, -ae, *f.,* switch, whip

virgō, -inis, *f.,* maiden, girl

virguncula, -ae, *f.,* little maiden, young girl

virtūs, -ūtis, *f.,* virtue, courage, worth, excellence

vīrus, -ī, *n.,* poison

vīta, -ae, *f.,* life; way of life

vitium, -ī, *n.,* fault, defect, vice

vītō (1), to avoid, shun

vīvō, -ere, vīxī, vīctum, to live, reside

vocō (1), to call, summon

Volcānus, -ī, *m.,* Vulcan, Roman god of fire and the forge

volō, velle, voluī, —, to wish, be minded

Volsiniī, *m.pl.,* Volsinii, a town in Etruria

voluptās, -ātis, *f.,* pleasure, delight

vorō (1), to swallow up, devour

vōtum, -ī, *n.,* prayer, wish

vōx, vōcis, *f.,* voice; utterance, word

vultur, -uris, *m.,* vulture

vultus *or* **voltus, -ūs,** *m.,* face, expression

zēlotypus, -a, -um, *adj.,* jealous